Ventures In Thinking

TEACHER SERIES

Constructive Communication and Structured Thinking in the Classroom

VOLUME 1

Ventures In Thinking
TEACHER SERIES

Constructive Communication and Structured Thinking in the Classroom

VOLUME 1

VENTURES EDUCATION SYSTEMS CORPORATION

Ventures In Thinking
TEACHER SERIES

**Constructive Communication and Structured Thinking in the Classroom
Volume 1**

ISBN 0-9716903-0-8

Printed in the United States of America.
10 9 8 7 6 5 4 3 2 1

Cover design and illustrations: Alexandra Leff

VENTURES EDUCATION SYSTEMS CORPORATION

15 Maiden Lane • Suite 200 • New York, NY 10038 USA
Telephone: 212-566-2522 or 800-947-6278 • Fax: 212-566-2536
Web site: http://www.vesc-education.com
E-mail: info@ventures.org

This volume has been a collaborative effort by the editorial staff of Ventures Education Systems Corporation. We acknowledge the following people for their originality and creativity:

Editor-in-Chief
Thomas Trocco

Senior Editor
Lorraine Janet Dean

Editor
Janice Novet

Writers
Katherine Schulten
Judith Gudgen

Production Editor
Barbara Beard

Graphic Designer
Alexandra Leff

Contents

PREFACE

We are all familiar with the frustration and confusion we sometimes feel when asked to recall or apply complex information. If the questions were framed in a different manner, we are certain our answers would be quick, informative, and would display mastery. In facing complex problems in subjects that are new to us, we are only too familiar with the sensations of being at a loss as to how to think about the problems and possible avenues for solution.

Fortunately, developments in cognitive science have provided understanding of how one learns and organizes information. These findings have resulted in practical applications and effective learning strategies that are easily taught and mastered by teacher and student alike.

Many of these strategies, particularly those emphasizing logical inference, analytical reasoning, and problem solving, comprise the Ventures Initiative and Focus® System of Student-Centered Learning. Explicit thinking strategies, coupled with techniques to enhance learned discourse and debate, are at the heart of the improved student performance and teacher satisfaction repeatedly reported in schools that have adopted the Ventures Initiative and Focus® system.

As an introduction to the Ventures Initiative and Focus® system of teaching and learning, this text provides explanation, practice, and practical application of effective thinking strategies. You will be exhilarated by the experiences of students of all ages as they become the masters of their own intellectual destiny in the classroom, and in life—confident in the efficacy of their own thinking and views and sincerely interested in those of their peers and colleagues!

Maxine Bleich
President

HISTORY AND BACKGROUND OF VESC™

Ventures Education Systems Corporation (VESC™) is an organization with more than 30 years experience working with educators nationwide to improve student learning, performance, and achievement. We serve educators and students in rural and urban schools of diverse populations, pre-K through 12th grade and at the university level.

Our work began in the 1960s, as a program of the Josiah Macy Jr. Foundation specializing in medical education. In order to increase the number of minority health practitioners, the program began with outreach and retention efforts in colleges and medical schools around the country. It soon became apparent that hundreds of young men and women were simply not graduating from high school and never going on to college. For these students, medical school was not even a possibility.

Known as the Macy High School Program, the foundation worked with some of the most poorly performing high schools in the country, both rural and urban. Among them were inner-city schools like DeWitt Clinton High School in New York City, which was about to be closed. VESC™ worked on the Navajo Reservation, where the teacher turnover is highest in the country, and the isolated schools in the Delta region of western Alabama and rural Arkansas.

In the United States, about one percent of college graduates go on to medical school—students who are generally male, white, and middle class. In contrast, more than 7% of the Macy High School Program graduates went on to medical school—*after* graduating from high school, and *after* four years of college! These extraordinary outcomes changed the lives of the young, minority men and women who were often economically underprivileged.

Because of the remarkable record of success resulting from the Program's student-centered instructional strategies, the Macy Foundation spun off the Program as two separate entities. The Ventures Scholars Program identifies high-achieving high school students from traditionally underrepresented groups and provides them with recognition, career information, and contacts with a consortium of undergraduate and professional programs in the health professions, science, engineering, and mathematics.

Ventures Education Systems Corporation, on the other hand, provides a school-wide pre-K to 12th grade professional development program. In addition to organizing the Macy instructional activities, the VESC™ system is built on recent developments in cognitive science and research on effective instructional practice.

VESC™ is the program in which you are now participating. It is a workhorse of a program—requiring nothing more than consistent and accurate implementation to improve student academic achievement. It is distinguished by its simplicity, its emphasis on Constructive Communication, the use of Structured Thinking Skills for the processing of information, and the sustained, in-class support that it offers teachers during the course of the three-year program. It requires no special materials, no additional staff, no reorganization of the school day; it is based simply on a change in instructional practice.

With the success of the Ventures Initiative and Focus® system, VESC™ became an active and visible participant in the education-reform movement. VESC™ is among the top three percent of models selected by K-12 schools in urban, small town, and rural areas, supported by the Comprehensive School Reform Demonstration program. VESC™ has received recognition from the U.S. Department of Education as a resource for the new high school initiative to create smaller learning environments in high schools that enroll more than 1,000 students.

Schools that have consistently implemented our instructional strategies have reported significant improvements in the academic performance of their students. These results stem from the conviction we share with the teachers with whom we work: That all students are capable of significant academic achievement and that the structured, student-centered techniques of the Ventures Initiative and Focus® system of Structured Thinking enable teachers to help students realize academic and career success.

*Education is the key to unlock
the golden door of freedom.*

— George Washington Carver

A Brief History and Background of the Teaching of Thinking

A mind is a fire to be kindled, not a vessel to be filled.

—Plutarch

A BRIEF HISTORY AND BACKGROUND OF THE TEACHING OF THINKING

1

Education, and an appropriate course of study for students, has been on the agenda for a very long time.

When new discoveries are made, generally the basic principles are defined first and then developed as technology and information related to the concept are explored. For example, Gregor Mendel outlined the principles of genetics in the 19th Century, many years before the technology was available for use in the exploration of the principles involved.

In the time of the Ancient Greeks, three hundred year or so BCE, the philosopher Plato proposed a course of study that included:

PLATO'S COURSE OF STUDY		
Content	**Purpose**	**Time**
Study of the exact sciences— arithmetic, plane and solid geometry, astronomy, harmonics	To familiarize the mind with relations that can only be apprehended by thought.	10 years
Followed by still severer study of Dialectic	To develop dialectic, the art of conversation, of question and answer— according to Plato, dialectical skill is the ability to pose and answer questions about the essence of things.	5 years

During this course of study students first learned facts, but more importantly they learned the relationship of the facts. Plato considered the determination of the relationship of the facts as thinking. The student next engaged in the still "severer study of dialectic," which continued for five years. This severer study of dialectic refers to the art of conversation, the ability to pose and answer questions about the essence of things. As Plato proposed, the dialectician replaces hypotheses with secure knowledge, and his aim was to ground all science, all knowledge on some unhypothetical first principle.

Aristotle laid out his ideas in a series of works that dealt with a universal method of learning. The purpose of these logical treatises was to develop a universal method of reasoning by which students can better understand the world.

The purposes of some of Aristotle's treatises are outlined below:

UNIVERSAL METHOD OF LEARNING ARISTOTLE'S LOGICAL TREATISES	
Treatise	**Purpose**
The Categories	Proposes a scheme for the description of particular things in terms of properties, states, and activities.
On Interpretation Prior Analytics Posterior Analytics	Examines the nature of deductive reasoning. Outlines the system of syllogistic reasoning from true propositions (categorical logic).
Metaphysics	Distinguishes among the four causes which may be used to explain everything. Explanation of why things are the way they are. Explains the role of chance in the operation of the world.
On the Soul	Explains functions and operations of all living organisms. Explains the use of sensation and reason to achieve genuine knowledge.

In recent times, it seems that the thinking required to establish the relationship of facts was largely ignored. Information was presented to students who then attempted to memorize information they did not understand. The fact that *each student* must go through the mental organization of information was largely neglected.

Even today, reference texts are accumulations of conclusions rather than a collection of original documents students can use to develop meaning and understanding. There was no opportunity to develop Plato's dialectical skills. Understanding did not need to be developed by each student, because the information had already been organized by someone else and presented to students.

Once again, however, the emphasis in education is on student-centered learning rather than on teacher-centered learning. Many individuals have further investigated the same principles described so long ago.

The national standards reflect an understanding that students need to pay attention to the type of thinking they use to organize content information. They also recognize the need for student to communicate effectively as they organize information.

The basic language of thinking has not changed since the time of Plato and Aristotle. The language used in today's national standards is much the same as the original language used by Aristotle and Plato, although now some of the types of thinking have been further divided into subgroups:

- classifying and categorizing

- describing

- defining

- sequencing or ordering

- cause and effect

- reasons and conclusions

- predicting

- making decisions

- problem solving

- communication

LANGUAGE OF THINKING THEN AND NOW	
Ideas from Plato and Aristotle	**New National Standards (Science)**
"…familiarize the mind with relations that can only be apprehended by thought."	"…use the cognitive and manipulative skills associated with explanations…"
"…given to the severer study of dialectic, the art of conversation, of question and answer…"	"…public discussions of the explanations proposed by the students is a form of peer review that helps students develop meaning and understanding…"
"…the dialectician replaces hypotheses with secure knowledge…"	"…important in inquiry is the establishment of an adequate knowledge base to support the inquiry…"
"…logic is the instrument by which we come to know anything…"	"…students must apply logic for their proposed explanations…"

The cognitive skills proposed in all national standards include:

The cognitive skills proposed in all national standards include the mental skills and processes listed above. These cognitive skills have their bases in the thinking described by philosophers long ago. However, each time a student learns to incorporate the cognitive skills to make meaning and to develop understanding of the world around them, they become new all over again. Everyone that uses the cognitive skills redevelops their joy of learning.

LINKING THE WORK OF PLATO AND ARISTOTLE
TO TODAY'S EDUCATION SYSTEM

It is true that from the time of Plato and Aristotle until today people have been considering, and trying to understand, the complex mental activity called thinking. There have been several ideas proposed regarding the nature of thinking and regarding whether or not everyone is capable of this mental activity. In fact, it is the idea that not everyone is capable of thinking that led educators to organize information and "deliver it" to the learner. Many dedicated individuals have spent years trying to dispel the idea that not everyone is capable of thinking.

No one, however, can deny the fact that a successful system of education is one that produces individuals who can communicate and can interact with others to organize the information that they encounter in both academic and non-academic settings.

An informed population is necessary for our country's governmental structure. It is students who must do the thinking to organize information, not educators. The types of mental exercise laid out by Aristotle are what will make the educational experience meaningful to the student.

LINKING THE WORK OF PLATO AND ARISTOTLE
TO TODAY'S CLASSROOM

This idea of setting up a classroom learning environment with the focus on thinking is new for many teachers and students. Beginning this process can initially present a challenge for both teachers and students. The techniques outlined in this book will help you begin the transition in your classroom. These techniques draw on the natural abilities of students that can be developed by systematic practice just as a physical ability must be developed by systematic practice. The operative word in both instances is the word, "systematic."

Students and teachers alike can engage in unstructured thinking practices in the classroom. In fact, one of the most common classroom occurrences is that students jump from on topic to another quickly, without systematically developing an understanding of the topic. While this may be engaging for students, it does not accomplish the ancient academic purposes of:

1. *"...replacing hypotheses with secure knowledge..."*
    —Plato

nor does it allow them to

2. *"...unify (each area of knowledge) them in a coherent system of thought by developing a common methodology that would serve equally well as the procedure for learning about any discipline..."*

    —Aristotle

nor is it consistent with the present-day belief that

3. *"...all students can develop the knowledge and skills...to learn, reason, think creatively, make decisions, and solve problems..."*
—National Standards Overview/Science

The techniques that you learn in this book will help you to ensure that students:

- learn how to organize their thinking.
- make their thinking explicit.
- develop communication skills to share their thinking.
- listen to the thinking of others.

The table below highlights how some of the VESC™ techniques could be used with some of the purposes of Aristotle's treatises.

LINKING THE VESC™ STRATEGIES WITH THE THINKING OF ANCIENT PHILOSOPHERS	
Ideas from Ancient Philosophy	**VESC™ Structured Thinking Strategies and Methods**
Plato's "dialectic"	Constructive Communication Verbalization Guidelines that achieve Effective Group Process Effective Group Process Discussion Developing an awareness of the factors that affect communication
Plato's "relations that can only be apprehended by thought"	Understanding the structure of the types of thinking, basic skills, and problem solving strategies Organizing facts using mental steps Understanding the purposes of the types of thinking and when to use each to build meaning and understanding
Aristotle's "...coherent system of thought...methodology ...for learning any discipline..."	Self-assessment of beginning understanding level Strategic use of mental skills and processes for building meaning and understanding The communication of meaning and understanding The independent development of questions that extend meaning and understanding

A systematic approach to anything is developed according to an underlying philosophy. Philosophy can be defined as a system of thought; a way of thinking. For example, if one is an optimist, all information is filtered through that system of thinking; if one is a pessimist, the same information is filtered through a different system of thinking. The platitude with which we are familiar is the optimist seeing a cup as half full and the pessimist seeing the very same cup as half empty. They have the same information but are using different filters.

"Culture" itself is based on a philosophy of thinking. One example of this is the mannerism of looking someone in the eye when speaking to them. Depending on the cultural content, this could be considered insulting, threatening, polite, or complimentary. The way of thinking—the philosophy of the particular culture—filters the act to give it meaning.

Again, a philosophy is a system of thought rather than individual facts, pieces, or opinions, and it is the system of thought that gives *meaning* to the individual actions (mental processing of facts, pieces, opinions) related to the system of thought.

This same system of thought can be applied to teaching techniques. Each interaction with students is viewed through one of the theories of learning (commonly referred to as behaviorist, cognitivist, and constructivist theories). The classroom applications of *intended* student-centered activities should produce higher student academic performance, and teachers are often frustrated when the activities produce no change in student performance.

The Ventures Initiative and Focus® System of student-centered learning integrates some aspects that sometimes cause no immediate change in student performance. It is an approach that accomplishes a System of Thought—a building of a classroom culture of thinking—related to a unique combination of teaching techniques. These include the Constructive Communication techniques of Thinking Aloud Paired Problem Solving, Effective Group Process, and Structured Thinking Skills.

The Ventures Initiative and Focus® System identifies the components of student-centered teaching techniques that should be integrated in order to improve student performance. If any one of the components is missing from the classroom application, then the student performance level is compromised.

- The explicit teaching of Structured Thinking will not significantly change student performance levels if the classroom environment is destructive in nature.

- A constructive classroom environment will not significantly change student performance levels if Structured Thinking is omitted from the instruction.

The integration of the two components produces a different System of Thought in both teacher and student. It is this different System of Thought related to learning that will produce significant changes in student performance levels. It is also this different System of Thought that creates a classroom environment necessary to accomplish the state and national standards for teaching and learning. Students create meaning and understanding of factual information using this System of Thought. They are able to retain and apply what they have learned, enabling them to become independent, lifelong learners.

Overview of the
Ventures Initiative and Focus® System
of Student-Centered Learning

Tell me and I forget.
Show me and I remember.
Involve me and I understand.

—**Chinese Proverb**

A LOOK AT TEACHER-CENTERED AND STUDENT-CENTERED LEARNING

For many of us, our mental image of school looks something like this:

> Thirty students sit in rows facing a teacher at the front of a room. The teacher writes information on the board and students copy it down. The teacher asks a question and five or six hands go up: the same five or six hands that went up the last time the teacher asked a question. The teacher then calls on one of those students to give the answer, and says, "Good!" when that student gives the "right answer"—the one the teacher wanted to hear. The teacher writes this answer on the board and the rest of the class copies it down.

If you visited some of today's classrooms, this is what you might still find.

Now contrast that approach to instruction with a Ventures Education System Corporation (VESC™) classroom:

> Thirty students sit in a circle. They are discussing a passage called "About Revenge," written by Francis Bacon. The teacher is simply sitting off to the side listening. The discussion is lively and occasionally emotional, but no one is raising a hand. Instead, students contribute as they would in a discussion that might take place in the real world—by making room for those who want to speak and refraining from distracting side conversations. A boy raises the question of when it is ever morally right to take revenge. Someone points out that in the passage Bacon notes that the government constantly takes revenge in the form of prison or capital punishment. "But is that different from individuals taking revenge on their own?" a girl asks, and there is a chorus of replies. At least 15 people have contributed so far to this discussion while those who have not spoken are listening attentively. As the discussion period ends, several students complain, "But I still had more I wanted to say."

How can educators get from the first scenario to the second? Can this second scenario occur only in elite private schools with honors students?

Ventures Education Systems Corporation believes that any classroom can be transformed from a place where passive and bored students wait for someone else to give "the right answer" to one in which engaged, excited students question, solve problems, and think independently. By practicing a few simple methods that help both students and teachers become aware of their own thinking and interaction, any classroom can change from a teacher-centered to a student-centered learning community.

In education today "student centered," and "active learning," have become buzzwords. Educators recognize that in the twenty-first century, information is constantly—sometimes overwhelmingly—available. An emphasis on merely recalling facts is neither practical nor useful. Information memorized for a test today is outmoded tomorrow. Instead, our children need to be able to organize, manipulate, analyze, and apply information of all kinds to a range of real-life problems. To prepare our students, we have to teach them to think and manage their own learning.

In most traditional classrooms nearly all of the questions asked are posed by the teacher—the one person in the class who already knows the answers. In a VESC™ classroom, student thinking drives the curriculum. Students ask the questions because they need to make meaning of information.

In a VESC™ classroom "student centered" does not mean unstructured. On the contrary, the Ventures Initiative and Focus® System works through a two-stage approach to make students rigorous in their thinking and responsible for making their thinking clear to others. By instructing students in constructive communication techniques and the simple structures for skillful thinking, VESC™ teachers give students the tools to learn independently.

For the VESC™ teacher, "student centered" does not simply mean that student desks are in a circle or that the teacher is no longer always at the front of the room. Instead, it means that all students have the ability and the responsibility to think for themselves and make meaning of the content they are learning.

The following chart illustrates some of the basic philosophical and practical differences between a traditional and a student-centered classroom.

CLASSROOM APPROACHES

STUDENT CENTERED	TEACHER CENTERED
Students are viewed as thinkers who come to the classroom with a body of knowledge and ideas of their own.	Teachers pour information into empty vessels, the students.
Teachers facilitate learning and encourage intrinsic rewards for academic and social development.	Teachers direct student behavior.
Curricular activities rely heavily on primary sources of data and manipulative materials.	Teachers feel responsible to cover the established curriculum.
Multiple sources, including students' questions and interests, are important for instructional planning and development.	Textbooks are major sources for instructional planning.
A more flexible use of time schedules.	Curriculum is tailored to fit given time schedules.
Student-to-student conversation and learning by doing are valued.	Whole-class instruction and teacher lectures predominate.
Key concepts, general principles, and the transfer of ideas across disciplines are emphasized.	The acquisition of facts and skills is emphasized.
By ongoing assessment, interwoven with teaching, teachers to plan next steps to meet student needs.	Assessment is separate from teaching and follows it in order to test students' retention of information.
Learning occurs through student–teacher, student–student interactions and learning by doing.	Quiet and order are valued as evidence of a productive and thoughtful classroom.

GOALS FOR LIFELONG LEARNING

In the student-centered learning environments that VESC™ helps educators and students create, students are able to develop the lifelong skills and strategies they need to be successful academically, in the workplace, and in our complex society. These skills include the ability to:

- learn how to learn

- participate actively in the classroom

- organize information to make it meaningful and useful

- read and write fluently

- read and write critically

- communicate constructively with others in any learning situation

- apply content effectively in problem-solving situations

- enjoy learning, in and out of school, now and for the rest of their lives

- feel confident in test-taking situations

- meet current and future academic challenges, in college and beyond, with confidence and skills

- know how to communicate their learning to others in speech and writing

- direct their own learning

This guide is designed to help incorporate the elements of a student-centered classroom into daily practice to implement a student-centered approach to teaching.

THE COMPONENTS OF THE
VENTURES INITIATIVE AND FOCUS® SYSTEM

The Ventures Initiative and Focus® System of Structured Thinking is composed of a unique combination of various methods and Structured Thinking strategies that can be used successfully the classroom. In this book, you will learn how to use them in a way that is student centered. They are laid out in the diagram on the next page. It is this combination that makes the system extremely flexible so that it can be used in any age group and with any curriculum content. As you become familiar with the techniques, you will see how flexible they are.

The Ventures Initiative and Focus® strategies and methods are indicated in the chart below.

METHODS	
Constructive Communication	
Thinking Aloud Paired Problem Solving	Chapter 3
Effective Group Process	Chapter 4
Assessing Prior Knowledge	Chapter 13
Structured Thinking Skills and Processes	
Making thinking explicit	All chapters
Graphic organization of information	Chapters 5–12
Metacognitive questioning	Mastery and self assessment sections in Chapters 3–12
Comprehension and Expression	
Comprehension and expression of Structured Thinking	Chapters 3–12
Literature Circles	Chapter 15
Author Study	Chapter 15
STRUCTURED THINKING STRATEGIES	
Comprehension Strategies	
Defining	Chapter 6
Describing	Chapter 7
Analytic Thinking Strategies	
Examining Similarities and Differences	Chapter 8
Analyzing the Parts of a Whole	Chapter 9
Categorizing and Grouping	Chapter 10
Ordering	Chapter 11
Supporting a Conclusion	Chapter 12

This book is the first in a series and is primarily concerned with Constructive Communication and the introduction of Structured Thinking.

Constructive Communication

In many traditional classrooms, student talk consists largely of giving answers when the teacher asks a question. In a VESC™ classroom, students constantly communicate with one another and the teacher as they make meaning of what they are learning. However, students in a VESC™ classroom also learn *how* to communicate effectively and constructively by practicing techniques specifically designed to help them do so.

Each student's ability to verbalize thinking and to listen to another's thinking must be developed if a teacher wants to establish a truly student-centered environment. Students cannot share information if they are unable to report accurately to others. Students will not interact in a group setting if they worry that they will be ridiculed, laughed at, humiliated, ignored, or talked over. Moreover, if communication is not constructive—if a few students dominate all class discussions, or if students are ridiculed for wrong answers—the whole class will respond negatively and performance levels will drop.

In short, no matter how effectively we teach students to think, students' academic performance will not significantly if they cannot communicate that thinking to others. Two basic constructive communication techniques are consciously taught and consistently applied in the VESC™ classroom: TAPPS and Effective Group Process.

TAPPS: THINKING ALOUD PAIRED PROBLEM SOLVING

Through paired problem-solving exercises, participants learn to articulate their thinking and to listen without interruption, except for clarification. This careful verbalization and listening clarifies thinking.

EFFECTIVE GROUP PROCESS

Students read and discuss specially selected texts while consciously following some simple guidelines for Effective Group Process. The teacher acts as facilitator, but students themselves run the discussion.

Structured Thinking

In recent years, many curricula have targeted student improvement in "higher order thinking." Yet though these curricula often provide interesting, one key component is usually missing: *Teachers ask students to do critical thinking, but they don't teach them how.* Students may have a creative learning experience, but they are still dependent on the teacher for structuring and guiding it.

In a VESC™ student-centered classroom, students actually learn the steps in commonly needed Structured Thinking Skills such as Examining Similarities and Differences, Ordering, Categorizing, and Supporting a Conclusion. For many students, this is the first time a teacher has shown them *how* to think skillfully, rather than just expecting them to know how on intuitively. Learning the steps of these skills gives students real self-sufficiency, tools to do these mental tasks they can use for the rest of their lives. If, for example, students know the simple steps in the Structured Thinking Skill of Examining Similarities and Differences, they are equipped to examine similarities and/or differences or answer any compare-and-contrast question in any classroom with any content. As they learn how to choose the appropriate thinking skill for different tasks, students become much more purposeful learners. They are not dependent on the teacher to make meaning of information for them, nor are they dependent on the teacher to tell them how to think about it.

In the traditional classroom the query, "What are you working on?" may be answered with one of the following responses:

"This exercise."

"I don't know."

"Maps."

"Something about sharks."

These students, still largely dependent on the teacher, are simply following directions with no understanding of why they are doing what they are doing. In contrast, students in a VESC™ classroom respond to the same question in a way that shows awareness of what they are doing and why. For example, an upper elementary school student might say:

"I am learning about nouns and verbs by using the skill of Examining Similarities and Differences. I've already listed similarities and differences and thought about how they are significant. Now I think that my conclusion will help me be sure that I know how to use them."

A high school student might say:

"I'm thinking about the major characters in this text. I'm using Ordering by Rank to do this. Right now I'm developing the criteria that I'll use to define what constitutes major characters, and I'll be ordering the characters in this text as determined by these criteria."

Structured Thinking Skills give students a powerful method for problem solving, analysis, and dissemination of information. Students who use these skills to process the content are also much more likely to retain that information than they would be in a class in which the teacher did the meaning making for them. Lists of memorized facts are useless unless students know how to apply them in unexpected contexts.

In other books in the series you will read further about Structured Thinking Strategies and Methods.

BRAIN-BASED RESEARCH AND THE VENTURES INITIATIVE AND FOCUS® SYSTEM

VESC™ strategies are grounded in research on how we learn. The work of Renate and Geoffrey Caine on how the brain takes in, uses, and remembers information is central to our constructive communication and skillful thinking. In the first year VESC™ works with a school, we concentrate especially on the following two research findings:

Preventing Downshifting and Promoting Long-Term Memory

Caine and Caine's research, described in *Making Connections: Teaching and the Human Brain*[1] and *Education on the Edge of Possibilities*[2] explains the importance of being in a state of relaxed alertness in order to learn. In this state learners perceive low threat, (they feel they are in a safe environment free from ridicule and humiliation) as well as high challenge. When learners are not in this state, "downshifting" will likely occur. Downshifting, according to Caine and Caine, is "a psychophysiological response to perceived threat accompanied by a sense of helplessness and lack of self-efficacy.... Downshifting appears to affect many higher-order cognitive functions of the brain and thus can prevent us from learning and generating solutions for new problems."

Constructive Communication techniques were developed by VESC™, in large part, to prevent downshifting. Students become aware of when and how their thinking is shut down, and learn strategies to fight it. Teachers learn how teacher-centered behaviors, such as giving automatic praise or censure for each student answer, can cause their students to downshift and stop learning. An environment in which every student is free to think at his or her own pace is carefully created and monitored.

Long-Term vs. Short-Term Memory

Along with an understanding of how to create "relaxed alertness" in the classroom, VESC™ teachers also learn how to teach to long-term rather than short-term memory. Caine and Caine in this area stress the differences between the two. Short-term memory contains those facts that have been "rehearsed" and memorized, such as phone numbers or facts learned just for a test. This kind of information is "linked to extrinsic motivation and is powerfully motivated by external reward or punishment." A behavioral approach

---

[1] Caine, R. and G. Caine [1994]. Making Connections: Teaching and the Human Brain. Dale Seymour Publications, Parsippany, NJ.
[2] Caine, R. and G. Caine [1997]. Education on the Edge of Possibility. Association for Supervision and Curriculum Development, Alexandria, VA.

to learning emphasizes short-term memory by stressing that students learn facts for tests rather than for deep understanding.

The information we store in long-term memory, on the other hand, is information that we understand deeply enough so that it becomes part of a mental map that we regularly and naturally use. As Caine and Caine express it, "... a student may memorize some math rules but find it impossible to use them when operating a cash register. That, in effect, is the difference between memorization and understanding. A preliminary definition of meaningful learning, therefore, refers to storage of items that have so many connections, and are of such quality, that they can be accessed appropriately in unexpected contexts."[3]

CHARACTERISTICS OF ROTE MEMORIZATION	CHARACTERISTICS OF HIGHER ORDER THINKING, BRAIN-BASED LEARNING, OR PROBLEM-BASED LEARNING
Requires repetition	Processed instantly
Limited in the amount of information	Unlimited in the amount of information it can process
Nontransferable	Transferable to other situations
Most is lost through decay in a short period of time	Information is retained
Uses little of the functioning capacity of the brain	Uses much of the functioning capacity of the brain

Students in a VESC™ classroom use a combination of Constructive Communication techniques and Structured Thinking Skills in order to make information meaningful. They learn to manipulate, analyze, and apply facts so that they are connected to these "maps" in our brains embedded in long-term memory. As with all VESC™ techniques, our goal is to equip students with tools for effective, lifelong, independent learning. Understanding how the brain works is part of this tool kit.

Focus on Mental Processing

During your first VESC™ workshops, you engage in some activities that focus on thinking and how to communicate your thinking. Similarly, VESC™ techniques and skills focus students on their thinking and the communication of their thinking. Together you and your students will create an environment in which they can freely share their

---

[3] Caine, R. and G. Caine [1994]. Making Connections: Teaching and the Human Brain. Dale Seymour Publications, Parsippany, NJ, pg. 47.

thinking. They no longer engage in classroom activities in which they try to guess what you want them to think. Rather than completing tasks without really thinking about and understanding the content, students use TAPPS, Group Process, and Structured Thinking Skills to process and organize curriculum content.

Meaning and Understanding

Throughout this book, we often refer to learning as *developing* or *creating meaning and understanding*.

Students develop *understanding* of a concept or topic as they engage with other individuals and with curriculum content. They develop the ability to know, comprehend, interpret, and explain what they have learned.

Students derive *meaning* through a social process: they continually derive meaning as they interact with the world and with the people in it. As students make meaning, their understanding of a concept or topic is modified by their prior knowledge, their experiences, and by the shared understandings of others around them.

VESC™ strategies and methods make the social nature of learning, meaning making, and the development of understanding explicit to students in the classroom.

Changing Practice in the Classroom

Making the shift from a teacher-centered to student-centered classroom requires significant changes in our behavior as teachers. The transition does not happen overnight. Indeed, changing behavior can be a slow and difficult process. Incorporating VESC™ techniques and skills into your lessons, however, will make this transition easier for both you and your students. Using the Structured Thinking Skills, TAPPS, and Group Process will bring about the change you want in your classroom practice.

KEEPING TRACK OF CHANGE

- Monitor how much time you are talking; it should be minimal.

- Try to remain neutral so that you really promote students' independence. They are not independent if they rely on signals and praise from you.

- Ensure that you do not shut down or direct students' thinking in particular ways.

- Because you will not be able to change everything that you do immediately, think about the amount of mental processing students are being asked to do and try to increase that every day.

- Encourage students to focus on the thinking skill or communication technique that they are using.

 POINTERS

> **Trust the process.** Students begin to rise to the challenge of independent learning when they see that the teacher will not do their thinking for them.

> **Do not think for students when they can think for themselves.**

> **Slow the thinking down.**

> **Keep the thinking going.**

> **Monitor students to ensure they do not shut down.**

> **Expect the change process to be messy at first.**

> **Remember to debrief new activities so students understand what happened.**

> **Give students frequent opportunities and guidance in self assessment.**

> **Validate works in progress.**

> **Surround students with student work.**

> **Be patient with students and with yourself.**

FREQUENTLY ASKED QUESTIONS ABOUT THE VESC™ PROGRAM

I have content to teach and standardized tests for which my students need to prepare. How can I add things like the Structured Thinking Skills, TAPPS, and Effective Group Process discussions and still have time to teach what is required?

You can incorporate the VESC™ skills and techniques and not lose time in addressing content because they are not "add-ons" to your curriculum. Instead, they are tools to help you do teach concepts, processes and principles better. VESC™ techniques are effective with any curriculum on any level. They help students process content more efficiently and with deeper understanding. To see this, select any day, week, month, or semester of your curriculum and find the points at which students should compare and contrast, sequence, solve a problem, or discuss an important issue as a whole group. Simply use a VESC™ skill or technique that will help students do each of these tasks with more structure, organization and self-confidence.

For example, your 11th grade English Language Arts curriculum may require three weeks reading and discussing a particular novel. You want students to understand the characters and their motivations, the main themes of the book, and the connections between this novel and life today. They must write an essay at the end of the three weeks that will trace one theme in the novel, a writing task worth one third of their grade. In the past, you have taught this novel through a combination of lecture, small-group activities, whole-class discussions, and individual journal writing.

Now that you know the basic VESC™ skills and techniques, however, you realize that the activities could be much more efficient if students use a Structured Thinking Skill or communication technique. For example, last year students in small groups discussed which character is the most important in the novel; this year you will make the same activity more structured by simply asking the groups to Order by Rank the characters, creating their own criteria for the ranking. Because they know the steps in the skill, they can be very efficient and thorough in prioritizing.

Last year class discussions usually involved only half of the class; this year students have practiced Group Process and can conduct a discussion using rules resulting in more student participation. Last year you had a free-form, large-class discussion about the differences between the hero and the villain in the story. This year, students can use Examining Similarities and Differences to compare and contrast the two characters and write and support a conclusion. Finally, at the end of the three weeks, students can approach the final essay question more skillfully using these same tools. They may first do a TAPPS on the question, orally listing their first ideas about the topic. They could then use the Structured Thinking Skill of Grouping to isolate the various themes of the book and the important scenes, quotes, and details that support this theme. They might then simply Order by Occurrence the points they want to write in the essay so that their final product is more coherent.

What if an administrator walks in while I'm practicing something like TAPPS and sees half the class talking at once? How do I explain what might look like chaos?

VESC™ only works in a school if administrators invite us to be there. These administrators should, whenever possible, also attend the training sessions so that they understand the techniques and can support their teachers. If questioned by an administrator, you can explain what TAPPS is and why it is done. You may also ask students to tell this visitor how TAPPS has helped them. Finally, you can show how this activity addresses many of the standards, especially those for speaking and listening, which appear in each subject area. If all else fails, you can meet with this administrator and the VESC™ trainer.

Can't I be teacher centered sometimes? For example, there are times in my curriculum when I need to give my students a lot of information, and lecturing is the most efficient way to do it.

We are all "teacher centered" sometimes, whether through long habit or because we have consciously chosen it as the most expedient method at that moment. However, we need to be careful not to believe that simply telling our students information means we have "covered" the content. Until they have processed it and made meaning of it, students unlikely to remember and apply this information. Therefore, though there might be times when you will lecture, you should use techniques to enable students to interact with the information before, during, and after the lecture. For example, if students need an overview of the causes of the Civil War, you may decide to give a short lecture in which they listen and take notes. Before the lecture they might be asked to do a TAPPS in which they list all the reasons they can think of that people go to war in general. During the lecture they may check off these reasons and write down the specifics that apply to *this* war. At the end of the lecture, students may form small groups to do a quick classification of the causes of the Civil War from their notes. While you have given them the information, they have the tools to make sense of it and think about its meaning.

I've been teaching a long time, and it seems like every couple of years there's a new "initiative" for schools. Haven't I seen this stuff before? And if it didn't work last time, why should I think it would work this time?

The Ventures Education System Corporation's philosophy and methods fall firmly in line with constructivist beliefs about teaching and learning that trace their origins to John Dewey. If you have been teaching for a long time, you have undoubtedly heard terms like "student centered" many times. You may already use many of these techniques.

We believe the VESC™ method is different, however, because it combines student-centered teaching and learning with cognitive tools to make learning meaningful. The effectiveness of the VESC™ method lies in the selection and combination of a few particularly effective techniques. Traditional and progressive teaching models advocate using critical thinking skills, just as VESC™ does. Teaching thinking skillfully allows students, not you, to do the thinking, that complex issues and challenging curricula require. Our model is also based on 20 years of research into what works with students at all levels to create independent learners and to raise test scores. As you try them you will see how dramatically this combination of methods can change your classroom and improve students' abilities to learn.

How soon will I see results from these skills and techniques?

If you follow the VESC™ processes carefully, you should see immediate results. The first TAPPS, Group Process Discussion, or Examining Similarities and Differences may not go as smoothly as it went in your training. Both you and your students need time to get accustomed to a new way of interacting. However if you try the techniques three or four times each, so that the method itself is no longer unfamiliar, students will surprise you with their thinking, understanding, and performance. You will see right away how eagerly students respond to being given both the freedom to think for themselves and the tools with which to do it. One high school biology teacher who used the VESC™ techniques to teach a unit on the human cell was amazed that on a standardized test over 90% of her students remembered and applied that information, whereas on the rest of the test, student answered only 50% correctly.

Thinking Aloud
Paired Problem Solving

*To be able to be caught up into the world of thought
—that is being educated.*

—Edith Hamilton

The Ventures Initiative and Focus® System begins with Thinking Aloud Paired Problem Solving (TAPPS). We teach TAPPS first because:

- it is enormously effective

- it's so simple that a teacher at any level can use it with students immediately

- it can be incorporated into and enhance many of the strategies learned subsequently

- it helps students clarify their thinking

- it demonstrates the value of verbalizing one's thinking process and listening to the reasoning of others

- it shows students the significance of reflective thought

- it promotes richness in students' responses regarding thinking and content

First described by Arthur Whimbey and Jack Lochhead in their book *Problem Solving and Comprehension[1]*, TAPPS was originally developed for use in solving problems in mathematics and English. In Ventures Education System Corporation (VESC™) training we use it to develop students' thinking, speaking, and listening abilities in all subject areas and at all levels.

In a TAPPS situation, two students are given a problem. One student is the Listener; the other is the Problem Solver. Problem Solvers "think aloud" by saying everything they are doing mentally to solve the problem. Listeners note everything the Problem Solver is considering and does to solve the problem. They are responsible for understanding the Problem Solver's mental process so clearly that they are able to report it back step-by-step.

While students are doing TAPPS, the teacher circulates among the pairs, listening to responses, but not interfering or offering judgmental comments. The teacher never gives "the answer," but instead uses this time to assess the extent which the whole class and individual students understand specific material.

---

[1] Whimby, A. and J. Lochhead [1982]. Problem Solving & Comprehension, Third Edition. The Franklin Institute Press, Philadelphia, PA

The technique allows students to express and explore ideas without being "shut down" by someone else—even someone else who is well-intentioned and trying to "help." Specific guidelines are followed, and students monitor their performance against these guidelines. After becoming comfortable with the technique, most students look forward to the freedom and creativity it offers; most consider it fun!

TEACHING TAPPS ENABLES STUDENTS TO:

- learn to communicate their thinking clearly to others

- learn to listen without interrupting or trying to "take over" the thinking of others

- are confident thinking for themselves

- learn to think through all kinds of problems without "shutting down" out of fear or reliance on the teacher or another student to do the thinking for them

- learn that there are many ways to approach and solve a problem and that others think differently than they do

- learn from each other how to solve common kinds of problems

- develop the ability to distinguish between the different mental activities of considering a problem, reducing their fear of considering a problem

- participate in Effective Group Process discussions in which they must share their thinking with a large group

- are prepared for Structured Thinking Skills because they are comfortable revealing their thinking and working through problems

- reflect on their thinking

- become competent in the communication standards required by the state standards in all subject areas

- have daily "minds-on" experiences solving problems related to content learning

WRITING TAPPS PROBLEMS: GETTING STARTED

You can create a TAPPS problem from any kind of content. Once students have mastered the technique, they will use it naturally and easily to address content in your class, in classes where TAPPS is not taught, and in their lives outside of school. Common kinds of TAPPS exercises include:

- working through test problems

- retelling the information in a difficult text after reading it silently

- explaining what is happening in a picture

- analyzing the information in a diagram or table

- giving an opinion on a controversial issue

- brainstorming possible ways to solve a problem

- planning or setting goals for a project

- processing other learning experiences, e.g. using the steps in a Structured Thinking Skill, identifying any new ideas or concepts

- reviewing material previously learned

- connecting prior knowledge to new learning

In writing the first TAPPS problems, remember that they should be challenging but not so difficult that students do not have a "way in" to solve it. The TAPPS activities should also be fairly short. In general, the best TAPPS problems either have multiple answers or multiple routes to an answer.

For example, a simple TAPPS problem may involve having students read a map and figure out the quickest way to get from one point to another. Though there may be one "best answer," the richest discussions take place when all pairs have finished their TAPPS and different students defend their route as the quickest. Avoid asking questions that elicit only a "yes" or "no." When creating TAPPS problems make sure that every student, no matter what level of ability can contribute to trying to solve it.

TEACHING TAPPS

First Step In Skill

Put students in pairs. One person is the Problem Solver, the other is the Listener. (See Appendix A for TAPPS guidelines for younger and older students.) Make certain before TAPPS begins that each pair knows who has which role and what that role entails. Also make sure they understand that the teacher will not give the class the "answer."

Second Step In Skill

Once pairs have been established and everyone understands his or her role, give out the TAPPS problem on a sheet of paper face down. When the group is ready, tell students to turn it over and begin, reminding the Problem Solvers to say everything they are thinking from the moment they turn the papers over, including reading the problem aloud.

As students talk, circulate throughout the room. Don't stop and obviously listen to any one pair. Be especially mindful not to intervene. Let students get comfortable with the technique since it will feel artificial and awkward the first few times they do it. *Do* try to listen to get a general sense of how hard or easy the problem is and to identify how individuals process it.

Third Step in Skill

After the group has finished, ask the Listeners to report back the thought processes of their Problem Solvers. This debriefing can be done first in just the pairs and later as a whole-group discussion. (In the whole-group discussion every Listener does not need to speak, since in most cases the process of the Problem Solvers will be quite similar.)

Common responses from Listeners after the first few TAPPS exercises include:

"He talked too fast for me to get it all."

"She forgot to say everything she was thinking, and when she got quiet I had to remind her to talk."

"He did it wrong; I wanted to jump in and tell him how to do it right."

Fourth Step in Skill

Next ask the Problem Solvers to talk about what it was like to have to say everything they were thinking as they solved the problem. (Again, it is not necessary to hear from everyone once the most common and important points have been made.)

Common responses from Problem Solvers after the first few TAPPS exercises include:

"It was hard to say everything I was thinking."

"I couldn't think and talk at the same time."

"I could tell my Listener wanted to jump in and tell me what to do and that drove me crazy."

"I was scared I wouldn't be able to solve the problem and I was embarrassed that the Listener would see that."

It is very important to analyze and discuss the exercise the first few times so that everyone sees that all have had a similar experience—that learning to think requires concentration and that learning to listen might be even harder. After the group becomes proficient, the class does not need to debrief every time in a large group. Instead, have the pairs simply turn to each other and assess how well they followed the Problem Solver and Listener guidelines. (See Appendix A for TAPPS self-assessments for younger and older students.)

POINTER: **Give students ownership of "the answer."**

A wonderful insight that happens after TAPPS exercises often comes out of the whole-class discussion. After puzzling through a problem, students nearly always want "the answer." Because the teacher is unwilling to give it, students are forced to look to each other to find it. Students' desire for the answer leads to the kinds of lively discussions of content teachers dream about and rarely get. For example, one student may spontaneously go up to the board to demonstrate her way to solve an algebra problem, while others argue that she missed a step. If the teacher truly stays out of this process, students begin to see that they can rely on their own thinking to understand even very difficult material.

INCORPORATING TAPPS INTO LESSONS

You can use Thinking Aloud Paired Problem Solving many times during the school day. Each TAPPS should be a short activity; once learned each may take no more than 10 minutes.

Most teachers' lectures can be adapted to successful TAPPS activities. A question or problem that arises out of the material can be written on the board. Rather than simply listening and copying down what the teacher says, students have a chance to grapple with the curriculum content and begin to make meaning.

An especially simple and useful way to use TAPPS is to close a class by asking students to take turns being the Problem Solver and Listener on the question "What do you remember from the lesson today?" A similar TAPPS can be used to open classes in which the content continues from the day before. Students who have been absent could be the Listeners in this case for an efficient way to "bring them up to speed" on what they missed.

VESC™ recommends teachers use TAPPS daily. It is the foundation for the techniques of Effective Group Process discussion and Structured Thinking.

TAPPS IN THE EARLY YEARS

TAPPS can be done with very young children. The TAPPS should be quite simple:

- counting the number of buttons in a bag or counting the number of children in a picture

- describing some of the things happening in a scene

- retelling a known story

- naming as many green things as they can think of

- doing a "book walk" through a story that they are about to read in a shared or guided reading session

At this stage, the goal of the activity is to give the children practice speaking and listening to a partner. To help them remember the rules, give the student who is the Problem Solver a picture of a mouth and give the ears to the Listener. (Pictures of an ear and a mouth are located in Appendix A, "Constructive Communication Resources.")

Young students may not verbalize all their thinking; just getting them to talk about what they are thinking is a big step. They are unlikely to ask questions for clarification and may find it hard to stay in role. Over time each child will develop as a Problem Solver and Listener.

Shy students will find speaking to a partner less intimidating than speaking to the whole group. Allow both students to be both the Problem Solver and Listener during the activity, having them switch roles after a few minutes. Keep the TAPPS activity short.

After the activity use Group Process and have students talk about what they did. Make sure that they are seated in a circular arrangement. Since in the TAPPS activity each child will have had the chance to think and verbalize he or she is more likely to have something to say in a group discussion afterwards. In this follow-up activity the goal is to talk about the activity that they engaged in, not unrelated activities.

SAMPLE TAPPS ACTIVITIES

MATHEMATICS

Number Sense
Describe all the places where you find the number three (four, five, ten, etc.).

How many legs are on a spider (or cow, boy, worm, etc.)? How many legs on two (three, five, ten, etc.)?

Money
Describe what you can buy with a dollar.

Geometry
Describe the following shapes: triangle, square, and circle.

Name all the things you know that contain a rectangle (cylinder, circle, cube, etc.).

Algebra

Write an equation for the following and solve it. The sum of twice a number and 17 equals 41.

Time

Clock A keeps perfect time, whereas Clock B runs fast. When Clock A says 6 minutes have passed, Clock B says 8 minutes have passed. How many minutes have really passed when Clock B says 56 minutes have passed?

Measurement

Name as many things as you can that are heavier than yourself (longer, shorter, younger, older, etc.).

Statistics

Tanya's scores on the first four of five 100-point tests were 85, 89, 90, and 81. What score must she receive on the fifth test to have an average of at least 87 for all the tests?

Fractions and Ratios

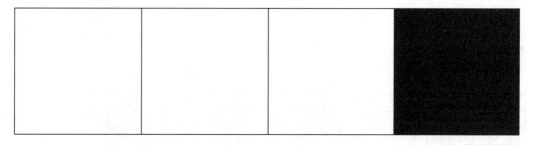

1. What fraction of the box is black? _____
2. What fraction of the box is white? _____
3. What is the sum of your two answers? _____
4. Complete this addition and subtraction:

   1/4 + 3/4 = _____   4/4 - 2/4 = _____

Dates

At what age did Benito die? He was born on April 24, 1911 and died on January 3, 1988.

Addition

Add arithmetical symbols between the twos to make every equation true. You may use plus, minus, times and divide symbols, as well as parentheses and brackets for grouping. (Ex: 2 2 2 2 = 0 could be written as (2 + 2) - (2 + 2) = 0).

2	2	2	2	=	0
2	2	2	2	=	1
2	2	2	2	=	2
2	2	2	2	=	3
2	2	2	2	=	4
2	2	2	2	=	5
2	2	2	2	=	6
2	2	2	2	=	10
2	2	2	2	=	12

Odd and Even

Explain to your partner what an odd number is and what an even number is.

Estimation

Mark has an average of 87 on the four tests he has taken. He could make the honor roll if he gets his average up to 90. There will be only one more test this marking period. What score will Mark need on the last test to give him an average of 90 for the marking period? Show your work.

Multiplication Table

	2	3	4	5	6	7	8	9	10	11	12	13	14	15
2	4	6	8	10	12	14	16	18	20	22	24	26	28	30
3	6	9	12	15	18	21	24	27	30	33	36	39	42	45
4	8	12	16	20	24	28	32	36	40	44	48	52	56	60
5	10	15	20	25	30	35	40	45	50	55	60	65	70	75
6	12	18	24	30	36	42	48	54	60	66	72	78	84	90
7	14	21	28	35	42	49	56	63	70	77	84	91	98	105
8	16	24	32	40	48	56	64	72	80	88	96	104	112	120
9	18	27	36	45	54	63	72	81	90	99	108	117	126	135
10	20	30	40	50	60	70	80	90	100	110	120	130	140	150
11	22	33	44	55	66	77	88	99	110	121	132	143	154	165
12	24	36	48	60	72	84	96	108	120	132	144	156	168	180
13	26	39	52	65	78	91	104	117	130	143	156	169	182	195
14	28	42	56	70	84	98	112	126	140	154	168	182	196	210
15	30	45	60	75	90	105	120	135	150	165	180	195	210	225
16	32	48	64	80	96	112	128	144	160	176	192	208	224	240
17	34	51	68	85	102	119	136	153	170	187	204	221	238	255
18	36	54	72	90	108	126	144	162	180	198	216	234	252	270
19	38	57	76	95	114	133	152	171	190	109	228	247	266	285
20	40	60	80	100	120	140	160	180	200	220	240	260	280	300

Explain how to use this table to count by tens from 10 to 100.

Explain how to use this table to count by fives from five to 100.

Use a marker to circle all even numbers. Explain why they are even.

Use a marker to circle all odd numbers. Explain why they are odd.

Use a marker to circle all the numbers that are divisible by five. Explain why.

Use a marker to circle all numbers that are perfect squares. Explain why.

ENGLISH LANGUAGE ARTS

Literature

Name as many stories as you can that contain bears (witches, wolves, a princess, a detective, a character from outer space, where the main characters are not human, a fight scene, a death, a tragic ending, are set in the future, the past, on a boat, in another country, in another land, etc.).

Describe all the ways our story could end.

Read the poem by Robert Frost called *Stopping by Woods on a Snowy Evening* and tell your Listener the following:

1. What is happening in this poem?
2. What do you think has happened just before the events or scenes in this poem?
3. What do you think will happen after the events or scenes in this poem?

This exercise can be used with nursery rhymes, songs, riddles, etc.

Writer's Workshop

Name all the words you can use instead of "said."

Describe all the ways you can make your descriptions more vivid.

Describe areas you'd like to work on in your writing.

Describe all the ways you can help someone else with his or her writing.

Scrambled Comics

Arrange the panels in a cut-up comic strip in order and explain your reasoning.

Grammar

In which sentence should you use "a" and not "the"? Tell your partner the guideline you developed for choosing which articles to use.

	Answer	Guideline
Where are _____ crayons Jack left on the table?		
David, do you have _____ favorite book?		
I often take care of _____ cats next door.		
Go to _____ basement and bring up my hammer.		

Facts and Opinions

Tell your partner the answer to each question. After each question, tell your partner the reason you chose the answer.

1. Which sentence is a **fact**?

   a. All bakers bake cake.
   b. Everyone loves cake.
   c. Baking is a fun job.
   d. Some bakers are old.

2. Which sentence is an **opinion**?

   a. Central Park opens at ten.
   b. Central Park has a zoo.
   c. The zoo is too crowded.
   d. People picnic in the park.

Letters and Sounds

List all the words you can think of that start with a certain letter, sound or prefix, or end with a certain sound, letter or suffix, or contain a certain sound or letter.

SOCIAL STUDIES/HISTORY

Civilizations

Below is a list of various civilizations and their accomplishments. Rank them in order from the most to the least important and explain your reasons for ranking them in that order.

- Sumerians: wheeled vehicles

- Hittites: ironworking

- Phoenicians: alphabet

- Persians: coins/money

- Babylonians: written code of law

- Hebrews: monotheistic religion

- Egyptians: calendar

New York City Subway Map

Use the New York City subway map to figure out how to get from the Bronx Zoo to the New York Aquarium (in Brooklyn) by way of Penn Station in Manhattan. Choose a route that is the fastest one possible using only the subway.

Cities and Populations

Atlanta has a larger population than Birmingham but a smaller population than Chicago.

1. Write the names of the three cities in order.

2. Verbalize every thought that occurs as it occurs.

3. Verbalize the thinking coherently to your partner so that your partner understands each step you take in the resolution of the situation, and the reason you took each step.

TAPPS Directions for Regents Preparation: Decoding the Question

1. If a diagram or graph is part of the question, explain to your partner what it shows. Label as many parts as possible.

2. Read the question. Underline the three key words.

3. Rephrase the question explaining what it is asking you to do. This includes defining all the words that are difficult or unclear. If you can, also identify what thinking skills or series of thinking skills it is asking you to use.

4. Now tell your partner the steps you would go through to answer the question or solve the problem.

SCIENCE

Elementary Science

List all the parts of the body that help you walk (help you digest food, help you think, help you see, smell, hear, touch, taste, etc.).

Describe all the parts of a magnifying glass (a bicycle, a telephone, a computer, a pencil, a calculator, etc.) and what they do.

Design an experiment to investigate what happens when you combine water and sugar (salt, food coloring, sand, coffee grounds, powder and beans, gelatin, wallpaper paste, etc.).

What's Alive!

You have been given a list of organisms for which you have to determine what would be the characteristics you could use to determine that they all belong to the category "living things." In choosing your characteristics you have to keep in mind that it (the characteristic) should be a characteristic of *all* the organisms on your list. The organisms include the following:

   fungi, leopard, fish, orchid, bacteria, lichen, human, algae

Earth Science

Explain these earth science statements.

1. The sun is closest to the earth in January, the middle of the Northern Hemisphere's winter, and furthest away in July, the middle of its summer.

2. The higher the altitude at any given latitude, the cooler it is.

3. Weathering produces soil.

4. During an earthquake, P-waves travel faster than S-waves.

5. Fossils are found in sedimentary rock, but not in igneous or metamorphic rock.

Physics

Explain these physics statements.

1. Although the acceleration due to gravity of any freely falling object near the surface of the earth is 9.8 m/s^2, a coin will hit the ground before a feather dropped from the same height at the same time.

2. Dancing on a nylon carpet can cause sparks to fly.

3. Sound from a rifle can trigger an avalanche.

4. A bat is seen hitting the ball before the crack is heard.

5. A straw appears to bend when placed in a glass of water.

Chemistry

Answer and explain these chemistry questions.

1. What mass of iodine-131 (half life eight days) remains 32 days after a 100 gram sample of this isotope is obtained?

2. How many calories are absorbed when 50 grams of water at 100° C are vaporized?

3. How many milliliters of 0.2 M KOH are needed to neutralize 20 ml of 0.1 M HCl?

4. The density of a gas is 1.96 grams/liter at STP. What is its molecular mass?

5. Which element in Period 3 is the most active nonmetal? Why?

Stranded!

Imagine you are stranded on a desert island and want to make a device for signaling passing airplanes. The only materials you have are a few long branches, a few pieces of clothing, some rocks, some matches, and a mirror. How could you put all or some of the materials together to construct a signaling device? Explain how each part would function.

Population Genetics

Below is a list of living things (organisms) that you will study this year. The list is arranged in alphabetical order. Why would it be too hard to learn about these organisms by starting with the name at the top and ending with the name on the bottom? What would be an easier way to learn about these organisms?

Amoeba	*Euglena*	Jellyfish	Robin
Bean	Fern	Lobster	Sandworm
Bread mold	Flounder	Maple tree	Shark
Chlorella	Frog	Moss	Spider
Corn	Geranium	Mushrooms	*Spirogyra*
Cow	Grasshopper	*Nostoc*	*Streptococcus*
E. coli	Human	*Paramecium*	Turtle
Earthworm	Hydra	Pine tree	Yeast

Chemical Compounds

Read the following paragraph to your partner. Construct a graphic organizer showing the hierarchy of the terms in the paragraph. Speak aloud as you create it.

Compounds are chemical combinations of two or more elements. Elements are comprised of particles called atoms, but elements cannot be broken down into simpler substances. Each atom has a nucleus, protons, neutrons, and electrons. Inorganic and organic are two types of chemical compounds. Salt, water, acids, and bases are some inorganic compounds. Proteins, carbohydrates, lipids, and nucleic acids are organic compounds.

THE ARTS

Visual Arts

Looking at this image, tell your Listener the following:

1. What is happening in this picture?

2. What do you think has happened just before the events or scenes in this picture?

3. What do you think will happen after the events or scenes in this picture?

Music

List all the instruments you hear in this piece of music.

List all the instruments in the string (brass, woodwind, or percussion) section.

FREQUENTLY ASKED QUESTIONS ABOUT THINKING ALOUD PAIRED PROBLEM SOLVING

Why can't I get my students to think aloud to their partner? They want to do the exercise and then say nothing!

Students have identified the most common reasons why they do not want to talk out loud. The reasons are:

- someone might laugh at me.

- someone might not understand.

- I might say the wrong thing.

- I don't know what to say.

Strongly reinforce the TAPPS rules until students realize that it is safe to think out loud.

How can I get my Listeners to participate? They sit and stare into space.

Encourage active listening by having the Listener use a simple graphic organizer to take notes as the Problem Solver speaks. The graphic organizer can be handed out or developed by the student.

How do I get my students to use words other than "you know" and "uh-uh"?

Be very patient and initially supply vocabulary liberally. Ask them what are they trying to describe and supply the content vocabulary they may lack at the moment. They will pick up terminology quickly.

My students say that they can't think and talk at the same time. How do I get them out of this mind set?

Use very short exercises in the beginning stages of TAPPS practice. Students must slow down thinking to be able to verbalize it. Reassure them that this may take time and require practice. They need to speak clearly and say each thought as it occurs. Focus on the verbalization process until they begin to be proficient at it.

Why can't I give students the answer after the exercise is over?

You want students to begin relying on themselves for answers. If they collaborate with their classmates, they will be able to reach an answer on their own, a much more satisfying experience for them than getting it from you. Not supplying one "correct answer" also prepares them for Group Process discussions and Structured Thinking Skills, in which the teacher also does not supply answers.

Effective
Group Process

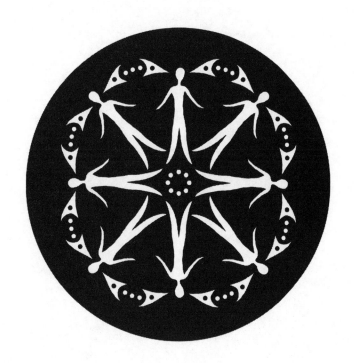

*...Individuals, working together, construct
shared understandings and knowledge.*

—David Johnson

Constructive Communication is a cornerstone of the Ventures Education System Corporation (VESC™) student-centered classroom. Thinking Aloud Paired Problem Solving (TAPPS) improves students' abilities to solve problems and communicate with a partner. The ultimate goal of a student-centered classroom, however, is for the *whole class* to be able to speak, listen, and think together as effectively as pairs of students learn to do in TAPPS. To achieve this, we use another technique: Effective Group Process Discussion. This technique teaches students to run their own lively and rich discussions without teacher intervention—important practice for independent learning.

Like TAPPS, the Effective Group Process Discussion method is quite simple. Introduce students to the "Rules of Group Process." These rules, such as "Listen carefully," and "Respond clearly to comments and questions" are sensible guidelines that members of any group, whatever age or background, must follow in order to have a profitable group discussion. The class then practices these rules by discussing a short selection that they read, view, and/or listen to (a text, photograph, painting, video etc.). The teacher does not guide the discussion in any way; instead, he or she acts as facilitator by ensuring that students follow the rules of Group Process.

These discussions provide a formal teaching session for practicing these rules. VESC™ recommends scheduling a formal Effective Group Process Discussion just once a week, but also providing opportunities for students to practice using these rules at many other times during the school day. Our goal is that students will follow the rules during *all* interactions in the classroom, whether discussing a story or textbook reading, reporting after a TAPPS, or simply talking informally in small groups.

The quality of Effective Group Process Discussions evolves quickly. As students become more experienced, they will begin to take responsibility for ensuring that their group discussion is meaningful. They will begin to monitor their performance against the rules of Group Process and comment when one of the rules is broken. When Group Process is working well, the teacher's involvement becomes minimal. Students become self-directed participants; less dependent on the teacher for "the answer," for praise, for encouragement, or for direction.

TEACHING EFFECTIVE GROUP PROCESS ENABLES STUDENTS TO:

- communicate their thinking clearly to others in a group situation without either dominating the group or "shutting down" and sitting passively.

- listen in a group situation without interrupting or trying to "take over" the thinking of others.

- listen to, reflect on, and respond to opinions of others.

- work with all participants, not just friends.

- take turns and become aware of other members of the group.

- ask when they do not understand something.

- think about questions for which answers are uncertain and become comfortable with ambiguity.

- give and receive constructive correction and criticism.

- admit that they are wrong without having this "shut down" their thinking.

- take on the responsibility of being a member of a group by contributing.

- realize that the teacher does not have all the answers, and that "student centered" means students think for themselves and share their opinions.

- do the efficient group work necessary for structured thinking.

- become competent in student academic standards for speaking, listening, and viewing.

- be more reflective, more motivated, and, ultimately, take on the role of classroom managers themselves.

Each student must develop the ability to work as a member of a group if teachers want to use collaborative learning in their classrooms. Students cannot share information and learn from each other if they are unable to speak and listen to each other. Equally important, students must be aware that the whole group must be involved and not just a dominant few.

Students will only work this way if an environment of constructive communication exists. They will not interact in a group setting if they fear that others will laugh at them, ignore them, or talk over them. The rules of Group Process help reduce these negative behaviors.

Because students listen to passages read aloud before the discussion begins, they are able to interact with texts that normally might be inaccessible to them. Through Effective Group Process Discussion they begin to make meaning of texts that otherwise would be far beyond their comprehension. They will also learn strategies that can help them when they individually comprehend a challenging reading passage, whether in school, on a standardized test, or in their lives outside of school.

Although some teachers are initially reluctant to take 30 minutes to engage in Effective Group Process Discussion, VESC™ strongly urges teachers to try it. Our experience has shown that student-centered change in the classroom is not possible without it. Students who have previously seemed bored or passive become engaged. Students will air ideas and opinions in this peer setting that a teacher could never have elicited. Students very quickly take on the responsibility for keeping the discussion lively and rich.

In an Effective Group Process Discussion, the interaction between students is the focus of the activity. When using the rules of Effective Group Process during other lessons, the curriculum content is the focus of the activity. The goal is effective content learning using meaningful discussion of complex or abstract material in a group setting.

These discussions lay the groundwork for a class of students who work together constructively. Remind students to practice the rules of Group Process as part of the regular classroom activity. Whenever possible take on the role of facilitator and ask students to address each other and think together according to these rules. The more often the teacher becomes the facilitator, the more students will take on the responsibility for their own learning.

TEACHING EFFECTIVE GROUP PROCESS DISCUSSION

It takes time to master the rules of an Effective Group Process Discussion and it is hard to follow those rules all the time. When people get emotional or frustrated they will shut down. The important thing is that the group does not allow Group Process to degenerate completely, and that students begin, individually and as a group, to manage this mental shutdown. Students experienced in the Group Process technique know that shutdown may result from internal factors, such as lack of interest in the subject matter, or from external factors, such as a teacher who keeps interrupting or irritation with a fellow group member. Mastery of this technique means that the group can identify any problems, deal with them constructively, and move on.

Student Outcomes with Effective Group Process Discussion

Mastery of Effective Group Process discussion will result in students who:

- sit in an arrangement that ensures that everyone can see and hear other group members

- stay focused on the material they are learning and engage in the learning activities presented

- maintain order in the group by controlling the impulse to speak while others are speaking

- follow the comments of others in the group as the discussion proceeds

- maintain a respectful attitude toward different perspectives

- respond clearly to comments and questions

- seek clarification in a way that keeps the communication constructive

- refrain from side conversations.

- take on the responsibility of participating.

- do not shut down but keep the thought process going.

- draw attention when the rules of Effective Group Process are not being followed.

If you give students a chance, you will find they have a great deal to say. Students may not always have wonderful discussions. As with any of these techniques, this process is a new way of interacting for many students and they must take them time to learn the process. *It is vital that you follow the guidelines and do not try to lead the discussion or help it along by asking guiding questions.* If you do this, students will not take ownership of the discussion nor think issues through for themselves. They will expect that, in the end, the teacher will do the hard work of thinking for them. Most students will remain passive. If you stick to the guidelines, however, after a few weeks students become quite involved and actively look forward to the discussions.

Introducing the Activity

The first step is to ask students to arrange the chairs in a circle. It is important that everyone can see everybody else's face. The first few times this shift may take longer than you hoped. However, as you all become accustomed to the process it will only take a minute or so.

Explain that you are going to give them a copy of a reading that you will read aloud. After you have read, you will ask them to write a question. It should be a genuine question that they have about the text. (Every honest question, including "What is this text about?" is a legitimate question.) Explain that you will choose a question, but will stay out of the discussion afterward. You will interrupt only to tell them that their time is up or to intervene if the conversation becomes too unruly for the group itself to handle.

Introducing the Effective Group Process Discussion Rules

Prepare the rules of Effective Group Process on the chalkboard, chart paper, or as handouts to students. (See Appendix A for Effective Group Process rules for younger and older students.) Review them quickly with students.

1. **Sit in a circle so you can see everyone.** Remind students that they must be able to see everybody's face since it is very hard to have a discussion with the back of somebody's head.

2. **Stay focused on the material.** As you read aloud, students will follow silently. The text will be the focus of the discussion that follows. Remind students that their thoughts and opinions are important during this process.

3. **Maintain order by controlling the impulse to speak when others are speaking.** It will be chaos if everybody is speaking at once. Nobody will be able to hear what others are saying.

4. **Maintain a respectful attitude towards different perspectives.** A true discussion does not consist of everyone just throwing in his or her ideas on the subject without taking account of what others have said. Exchanges should be respectful and constructive.

5. **Listen carefully as the discussion proceeds.**

6. **Respond clearly to comments and questions.** Everyone should speak loudly and clearly and listen to what other members of the group have to say.

7. **Seek clarification in a way that keeps the communication constructive.** There should not be arguments; rather, students should ask each other for clarification. (For example, "Where in the text does it say that?" "Why do you think that?" or "I have not found that to be the case, my experience was...")

8. **Refrain from having side conversations.** Anything that is said should be said to the whole group.

9. **You have a responsibility to participate.** When students are assessing the discussion, they will probably address the extent to which everyone has participated and how this affected the richness of the conversation.

The Reading or Stimulus for Discussion

The stimulus for the discussion may be a reading, a picture or photograph or video or film clip. If you are using an image, make sure that everyone can see it clearly. Give students time to study it carefully and write a question.

If using a text, give each student a copy of the reading. Remind them all they will write a question about what they have heard. Read the selection aloud and give students time to write the question.

Explain that the question should be short and one for which they do not have an answer. It is important that they write down the question or they will not remember it exactly if it is the one chosen. Once students have stopped writing, ask them to share their questions. As students read their questions, listen carefully. Do not spend time recording the questions; this distracts the flow of the process. If some students do not have a question, remind them that you will come back to them at the end. If some students state an opinion rather than a question, ask them to rephrase it in the form of the question.

Choosing the Question

As you listen to the questions, note those that may prompt student discussion. Questions that have no single answer and those that sum up what many students want to know work well for discussion. Simply phrased questions nearly always work, because everyone can readily understand them. After the first few discussions, some teachers decide that it does not matter which question they choose; the group will soon understand that it can take over and redirect in their discussion if it falls flat.

Refrain from giving students any type of valued response such as, "Samara's was a good question, let's start with that." Just say, "We are going to take Samara's question." Ask Samara to read her question again and say something about why she wrote it. Then wait for students to start talking.

Hold an Effective Group Process Discussion every week. Make sure that you choose questions posed by different students.

The Discussion

You really must keep out of the discussion. Make a conscious effort to refrain from commenting. Initially students will probably talk to you or look to you for signals that they are saying or doing the right thing. Do not establish eye contact with the student who is talking. He or she should be talking to the group, not the teacher. Look at the group but avoid catching anyone's eye. Keep your facial expression very neutral. Although students may look to you for indications as to how they are doing, give them as few hints as possible.

This technique plays an important part in making the shift from a teacher-centered to student-centered environment. Once again, students must think and respond without depending on praise or other responses from the teacher.

At times, there will be silences, particularly in the early stages. Just wait out these pauses. If you step in and stop the discussion, or pose questions yourself, the group will wait for you to step in every time. After a few discussions, students will begin to see that you really are not going to intervene and there will be fewer silences. Silences that do happen will indicate that students are thinking about what they have discussed and formulating an appropriate response.

If Group Process continually breaks down, you can stop the discussion. Many of students may be disappointed. Just explain that the activity is over for that day and the group will have other discussions soon.

If someone says that he or she is playing the role of "devil's advocate," explain that this does not follow the rules of Group Process. Individual's own opinions are important, not what they think somebody else's opinion might be.

Very quickly, students will begin to comment whether they are following the rules of Effective Group Process. Initially, however, you may have to comment if there are side conversations or interruptions. Just say, "The rules say no side conversations." Do not say, "Paul and Steven are having a side conversation." They will be well aware that they were the ones breaking the rules. After 15 minutes or so, end the discussion. Just say, "Our time is up. Let's spend a few minutes talking about what happened and whether the rules of Group Process were followed." Do not ask anyone to conclude the discussion.

Assessment of the Discussion

Give everybody a copy of the Effective Group Process Self-Assessment handout (found in Appendix A.) Have the group assess the discussion against the rules. They may talk about themselves or about the group as a whole. The rules of Group Process still apply during the assessment. You may find that students who did not participate in the main body of the discussion may join in at this stage.

During the initial assessments, students' comments will probably focus on aspects such as side conversations and interruptions. They may also discuss the rule that states, "You have a responsibility to participate." Many groups have interpreted this principle to mean that students must listen and be engaged, but may not always choose to speak.

Students sometimes become complacent in the assessment phase. They may become self-congratulatory, insist that they have followed the rules, and be resistant to further discussion of the process. When this begins to happen, introduce the student to the Effective Group Process Self-Reflection questions in Appendix A, "Constructive Communications Resources." These guidelines will help students clarify what happened during the discussion. They may also help improve Group Process.

A Quick Guide to Student Behavior Using Effective Group Process Discussion

Before the discussion, students:

- arrange themselves in the appropriate seating arrangement quickly and quietly.
- actively listen to and/or view the material carefully.
- formulate a question for discussion based on the material.
- read their question loudly and clearly.

During the discussion, students:

- maintain order in the group by controlling the impulse to speak while others are speaking.
- remember the comments of others in the group as the discussion proceeds.
- maintain a respectful attitude toward different perspectives.
- respond clearly to comments and questions.
- seek clarification in a way that keeps the communication constructive.
- refrain from having side conversations.
- keep thinking and working with the group even through rough patches in the discussion.

After the discussion:

- honestly assess the discussion in terms of how the group followed the rules of Effective Group Process Discussion.

Responses During or After an Effective Group Process Discussion

In all discussions, you must trust the process. Always expect the group to deal with its own issues. Students will not see the session as an opportunity for authentic discussion if, every time the situation gets difficult, the teacher takes over. Some of the discussions detailed in the following text are very difficult while others are wonderful moments that you will remember forever. When they happen, there is often a real breakthrough in how well the group works together.

SILENCE

Remember: Silence is okay. Many times in life, we have to deal with awkward silences. Students should work out how to handle such situations. You may be surprised how gracefully they do so!

EMOTIONAL DISPLAYS

Comments may strike an emotional chord with someone and he or she may become angry or tearful. There are many times in real-life conversations when this happens. Effective Group Process Discussions often resemble authentic conversations much more than "school discussions." Let the group deal with this, too. Afterward you may choose to speak to the student privately.

STUDENTS REFERENCE EARLIER DISCUSSIONS

A student might say, "This reminds me of the character that we read about in the Kafka piece." You will probably glow with pride, but remember to stay neutral.

THERE IS A "REVOLT" IN WHICH NO ONE UNDERSTANDS THE READING

The group should find a way to handle difficult material, perhaps by focusing on a starter question like, "What is this text about?" When working effectively together, a group may ask the teacher for references, dictionaries, or advice. As facilitator, you can help without compromising students' abilities to solve problems for themselves. If they cannot move from their frustration with the text into any kind of useful discussion, you should use the assessment phase to talk about what happened, why, and how it can be different the next time.

THE DISCUSSION CONTINUES AFTERWARD, IN THE LUNCHROOM OR EVEN IN ANOTHER CLASS

Sometimes the compelling issues raised in a discussion are common concerns or controversies that people have talked about over long a period. The discussion obviously piqued students' intellectual curiosity. Consider letting them extend some of their questions or insights into research projects or writing.

SOMEONE FEELS "UNCOMFORTABLE" EITHER DURING THE PROCESS OR AFTERWARD

Occasionally a student may feel uncomfortable or even emotionally threatened during a discussion. Dealing with strong interactions is part of the learning process. Both the group and the individual will grow from the experience, if they discuss it in the appropriate assessment phase.

STUDENTS MAY SHARE PERSONAL EXPERIENCES OF FEELINGS WITH THE GROUP

Try to remain neutral and let the group handle it. You might choose to remind the class that anything said in a discussion should remain confidential within the class. You may also speak to the student privately afterward.

Making Progress with Effective Group Process Discussion

Once students understand that they are in charge of making their own Group Process effective, this type of discussion is a wonderful activity. When students first learn the technique, however, you may need to set some specific goals and standards.

1. Students should move the furniture quickly and quietly to form a circle. Time the group and prompt them to improve the speed at which they do this task.

2. Initially not everyone may write a question. You can comment that often the simplest questions are the ones that start an effective discussion. If they seem stuck, encourage students to write the first question that comes into their minds. Review this part of the process during in the assessment section. If all students offer a question, then everyone was participating at this stage in the process.

3. After a few weeks, some students may still not contribute while others will continue to be very dominant. Without making it obvious, ask some of these students to sit outside the circle to observe and comment on what they see. Ask each student to monitor a specific rule, for example, the level of participation or the number of interruptions or side conversations. During the assessment process, ask them to share those observations.

4. You can also ask students to record response patterns by writing notations or marking on a circular diagram. This will document whether a few individuals dominated the group or indicate individuals that did not participate at all.

5. After a few weeks, you will really see students begin to make progress. They will also practice what they have learned about communication in other classes. When you teach the Structured Thinking Skills, you will once again be in the role of facilitator, though instead of a text selection, students will discuss curriculum material.

INCORPORATING EFFECTIVE GROUP PROCESS DISCUSSION INTO LESSONS

When beginning to teach Group Process it is very important to remember the focus of the activity is the group interaction, not the text or stimulus itself. If the text is a piece of curriculum material, it will be hard to focus on the Group Process and not the content so it is often easier to take a text that does relate directly to curriculum content. Choose a stimulus that generates some type of emotional response in the reader. Well-chosen newspaper articles, fables, classic texts, or topics that raise issues can lead to particularly successful discussions. You can also select an image or piece of film or video. Some suggestions of topics are outline below:

POSSIBLE TOPICS FOR DISCUSSION	
Grade Level	**Possible Topic**
K-2	<ul><li>short readings on the roles of police officers, firefighters, community workers</li><li>scary sounds</li><li>too much candy</li><li>saying please and thank you</li><li>me first, always</li></ul>
3-6	<ul><li>history of my neighborhood</li><li>state history</li><li>who to invite to my birthday party</li><li>principles of family organization within communities</li><li>games I like to play</li></ul>
7-9	<ul><li>rights and responsibilities as a U.S. citizen</li><li>local environmental issues</li><li>space exploration</li><li>morality of cloning</li><li>nuclear disarmament</li></ul>
9-12	<ul><li>organic farming</li><li>pollution control</li><li>species and habitat preservation</li><li>responsibilities of businesses</li><li>making choices as a voter</li></ul>

Effective Group Process Discussion in the Early Years

Establishing Constructive Communication and Effective Group Process Discussion is a worthwhile goal of any teacher, whatever the age of the students. For many children, starting school is the first time that they have had to communicate in a large group. Teachers of young students can use a variety of methods to encourage children to speak and listen to each other in a group situation.

To begin the process of teaching Effective Group Process Discussion, ask students to sit in a circle. Sit or kneel at about their level. You can also kneel behind the child who is talking to encourage students to talk to each other rather than to you, the teacher. Encourage them to speak loudly and clearly so everyone can hear. Discuss being a good listener. At the end of the discussion or activity, ask students if they think their classmates listened well, joined in, and spoke loudly and clearly.

Many picture books you can use in read alouds can raise issues that provoke thoughtful discussions for young children.

You can also use simple songs or rhymes that students sing or say together as a whole group. Then, students can choose and say rhymes or sing on their own or in small groups. Then, introduce rhymes or games in which each student has to make an individual response. Here are some examples:

- "Who stole the cookies from the cookie jar?" In this song, each student has the opportunity to say "Who Me?" "Couldn't be!" and nominate the person sitting next to him or her.

- "Telephone." The teacher whispers something in a child's ear and students pass the message around the circle. At the end, the last person shares what he or she heard and everyone laughs at how different it is from the initial sentence.

- "I went shopping and I bought a ____," or "I went to the zoo and I saw a _____." Each child has to extend the list. The first child says, "I went to the zoo and I saw an elephant." The second child says, "I went to the zoo and I saw an elephant and a monkey." The third child says, "I went to the zoo and I saw an elephant, a monkey, and a lion." Initially, ask students to repeat only what their immediate neighbor says, since remembering the whole list can be difficult.

- Retelling a story that they all know well. Have students go around the circle and contribute a sentence to the story. This may lead to discussion as to the events in a story.

- Creating a story in which each child contributes a word. For example, as a morning routine, students can share some news or say something about what they are going to do that day.

- "I Spy" is another game that requires students to listen and talk.

Schedule these activities several times throughout the day. They are a good way to begin and end the day and work well after recess. Once younger students are participating readily, they can talk about a picture or interesting objects or music. Sometimes you can have students share questions they have about a picture or object.

Encourage them to talk and see if they can answer any of the questions that are on the board.

Moving from the Teacher-Centered to Student-Centered Classroom

Effective Group Process Discussions give you the opportunity to practice the role of facilitator in a student-centered classroom. As with TAPPS, remember to trust the process and allow students to think.

Sometimes, students do not comply with the rules of Group Process. They interrupt or disagree in manner that is not respectful. Initially you may remind them of the rules and encourage them to monitor their own behavior regarding these rules. As the classroom becomes more student centered, they will have "absorbed" the rules, and will follow them naturally.

No matter what kinds of grouping—alone, pairs, small groups, or the whole class together—your class will constantly hone its ability to work together constructively.

FREQUENTLY ASKED QUESTIONS ABOUT
EFFECTIVE GROUP PROCESS

My students want me to tell them a question to ask. How do I get them to formulate a question in response to the reading?

Initially, use very short readings that are familiar to them. The reading should concern a topic that is common to their experience, such as the reading on revenge.

My students want to give an opinion rather than ask a question for discussion by the group. How do I get them to ask?

Have students rephrase the opinion as a question. Rephrase statements such as "I do not agree that all teenagers are rebellious." Say instead, "Why does the author think that all teenagers are rebellious?"

What do I do when one person does all the talking?

Because appropriate intervention techniques are difficult, they take practice. In the beginning discussions there are often many problems to address. The domination of the conversation by one or several students is a common problem. The easiest solution is to appoint one or two students as Group Process evaluators. These students will record who speaks and how many times each person speaks. The evaluators use a list of group participants and simply check the list as each individual speaks. The compiled list will indicate whether or not a group is functioning, or whether there are only a few individuals participating.

What do I do when my students have no idea what the article is about?

To make students more comfortable explain that "What is the author talking about?" is a very valid question and one that we all use often. Discuss the article paragraph by paragraph until students begin to establish a familiarity with the topic.

My students will not talk about the topic if they have an idea that is contrary to the perspective of the author of the article.

Encourage students to examine the reasons for the author's perspective and the reasons for their individual perspectives. Remind them that the purpose of one exercise is to communicate with individuals whose views are different.

Can I use my curriculum content when I am first teaching Effective Group Process? I don't have time to devote to readings that aren't in my curriculum.

Eventually you will regularly use your own content for Group Process discussions. When you begin Group Process discussions, however, you should use a stimulus that does not have a direct relationship to the curriculum content so that you can focus on the interaction rather than the content. Remember that initially you teach Effective Group Process to improve communication, not to teach content.

Using a reading from your curriculum, students may not be able to concentrate fully on the Group Process. Instead, they may worry that you were assessing their responses, and wonder whether the passage will be "on the test." You may be distracted by trying to evaluate whether students understood the content well enough, or planning how the discussion would fit best with what you will be teaching next. Your first Effective Group Process discussions work best if they are divorced from your content objectives.

Introduction to the Teaching of Structured Thinking Skills

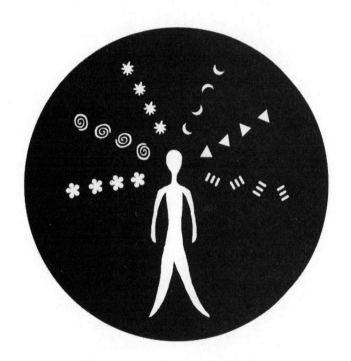

They know enough who know how to learn.

—Henry Adams

INTRODUCTION TO THE TEACHING OF STRUCTURED THINKING SKILLS

5

Standardized tests, textbooks, or curricula today increasingly ask students to "think critically." In every subject area and at every level, schools demand that students apply information and that is to analyze, predict, infer, or draw conclusions about its meaning. The New Standards Movement has been instrumental in making this kind of "higher order thinking" a requirement for graduating from high school.

Yet, few schools explicitly teach their students how draw informed conclusions using the information and ideas in the curriculum. While, we may ask students to "compare and contrast" or "analyze," teachers often assume that they naturally know how.

In a VESC™ school, students *learn how* to think critically. They understand that skillful thinking has a structure: a set of steps that logically work in sequence. VESC™ students learn the structure of the common Structured Thinking Skills and how to apply them to all kinds of information. Effective thinking skills then become tools learners can use all their lives, regardless of the material, circumstances, or teacher.

For example, students who learn the simple steps for analyzing the parts of a whole can then use those beyond the science class where they learned them. They can also analyze how the parts of a poem form the whole thought, how the elements in an equation function as a mathematical statement, and how to fix the broken parts of a digital camera.

Chapters 6 through 12 introduce the basic Structured Thinking Skills of the Ventures Initiative and Focus® system:

- Describing and Defining
- Examining Similarities and Differences
- Analyzing the Parts of a Whole
- Categorizing and Grouping
- Ordering by Time, Rank, and Occurrence
- Supporting a Conclusion

We already use all the Structured Thinking Skills. Our minds have been naturally using them since we were born. While we have no trouble "comparing and contrasting" two outfits to decide which to wear in the morning, many of us would probably have considerable trouble if asked to compare and contrast quantum and classical mechanics. Discrimination is difficult because we do not know enough about these two kinds of mechanics. Even using a resource on mechanics, however, many of us would not know what to do in order to draw a conclusion about the relationship between quantum and classical mechanics. A student who knows nothing about mechanics but does know the steps in the Structured Thinking Skill of Examining Similarities and Differences, however, will be able to read this resource skillfully and use the information in it to make meaning. This student knows *how* to learn.

Consider the following tasks commonly demanded of students:

- Determine the pivotal battles of the Civil War and explain your reasons.

- Compare and contrast an animal cell and plant cell and reach a conclusion regarding the major differences between the two.

- Describe the role of each of the branches of the federal government and the relationship among them.

- Identify a major theme in this novel and give reasons to support your answer.

In a traditional class, the teacher may "cover" the information for these tasks by writing notes on the board or assigning a textbook chapter. Students then work quietly and alone to provide written answers to these prompts, using their texts and notes as a resource. At the end of the period, students would hand in their answers to be graded.

In this scenario, able students may have very little trouble, since they already know how to skim a textbook, identify the information they need, and copy it. Less able students, however, would probably sit silently and passively, unsure where or how to start. Most students, regardless of whether they got the "right answer," may not remember this information and be able to apply it in a new or creative way a month later.

By contrast, students in a VESC™ class assigned exactly the same tasks would approach them quite differently from the beginning. First, rather than look for a prepared answer from a textbook or notes, they would identify the thinking skill that the task requires. Once they had determined the kind of thinking they should use, they work alone, in small groups, or as a large class to think through each step of the skill. As they consider each step, they would go to the teacher, textbook, or another resource to get needed information. In the end, each student writes his or her own conclusion or summary statement.

For example, an 11th grade social studies class might approach the first question ("Determine the pivotal battles of the Civil War and explain your reasons") by, as a class, deciding that the skill of Ordering by Rank was the most appropriate to use. They might then together perform the first two steps in the skill and determine the reason and criteria for the ranking. Students might then work in small groups with resources to discuss together which battles fit those criteria. Each small group might then share its answers with the whole class. If there were different responses regarding the significance, students might use Effective Group Process to discuss the reasons for their different choices.

These students are not dependent on the teacher to either tell them what to do or to give them the answer. Because they used information and made it meaningful rather than simply copying it down, they are much more likely to remember it. Less able students are also much less likely to "shut down" because they can seek help, and because there is not a set time limit at which the "right answer" is expected. When these students must evaluate possible causes of global warming in science class, they will know exactly what to do, even if that teacher has never heard of "The Structured Thinking Skill of Ordering by Rank." At the end of the year, when they take a standardized test in English, in which they must write an essay describing how a specific place influenced an author's life and work, students could once again use the skill of Ordering by Rank to organize their writing.

TEACHING STRUCTURED THINKING SKILLS ENABLES STUDENTS TO:

- Slow down their thinking so that they are systematic and accurate.

- Use powerful tools for problem solving, analysis, and dissemination of information.

- Increase their capacity for retaining information.

- Have greater confidence in any learning situation, including tests and activities involving challenging content.

- Organize *any* kind of information to make meaning.

- Increase their reading comprehension and writing fluency.

- Make their writing more purposeful.

- Develop their vocabulary.

- Be independent learners.

- Acquire these skills as lifelong assets to use in their education and the workplace.

When students know the Structured Thinking Skills needed to perform well in required classroom tasks and on standardized tests, they gain greater confidence. This internal confidence continually develops as students become more confident and competent learners.

Once they apply Structured Thinking Skills independently, their academic efforts become more time effective and productive. They organize information and ideas meaningfully and feel secure in their own ability to organize, retain, and apply information, rather than relying on rote memory of what someone else said. Independent, systematic use of Structured Thinking Skills engages and motivates students, even when the topic is not one of the student's favorite subjects.

TEACHING A NEW STRUCTURED THINKING SKILL

When first teaching a skill to students, do not spend a great deal of time describing it. Instead, go straight to the process and let students experience using the skill.

Use the skill with simple content; something with which students are familiar. Use everyday examples like apples, a table, or a set of buttons—whatever makes sense for the skill that you are teaching.

Introducing a Structured Thinking Skill

1. Tell students the name of the skill and ask them to locate it on the Ventures Initiative and Focus® System of Structured Thinking.

2. Present the mental steps of the skill.

3. Demonstrate how to lay out the steps graphically using the graphic organizer as a guide. You may hand out a copy of the appropriate graphic organizer from the VESC™ *Teacher Resource Guide*.

4. Take students through every step of the skill. When a skill is new, work with the whole class. As they become more familiar with the process, they will work through a skill individually, in pairs, or in a small group.

5. Make sure that students write during the process. Ask students to summarize the information graphically in their own notebooks. Explain that students may add to or alter what they have written as they hear what their classmates say. When working with very young children, the teacher organizes the information as students verbalize it.

6. Ask students to verbalize their complete thoughts and attempt every step of the skill.

7. Remember your role: Stay neutral and just facilitate the process. Write down exactly what students say and be sure to accept all responses.

8. Make sure that students follow the rules of Effective Group Process. Everyone's contribution should be listened to, valued, and there should be no sense of ridicule.

9. Make sure that every student writes a summary statement or interpretation. Students often think they are expected to write one given answer or that other students have a better conclusion than they do. With experience, their conclusions will become more sophisticated.

10. Ask students to share their written summaries or interpretations.

11. Give students time to look over their notes and refine their summaries or interpretations after hearing those of others.

12. Ask students to review the mental steps that they went through in TAPPS pairs or in small groups.

What Teachers Do During the Process of Teaching Structured Thinking

The teacher facilitates discussion of the steps in the skill and ensures that students follow the rules of Effective Group Process. Arrange students so that they can see and hear each other's responses.

As with the Constructive Communication techniques, teachers remain neutral during the teaching of structured thinking. They do not make value judgments regarding students' responses. You can thank them for their contribution but train yourself not to say things like "great idea," "good answer." This can act as a shut down to the student who may think, "My response is different to that and not as good."

At many times during the early stages of teaching a Structured Thinking Skill the teacher will act as a scribe. You need to write down exactly what students say. If you begin to change or paraphrase what they say, some students may shut down, thinking that they do not know what you want. Others may not share their thinking but give responses that they think you want to hear. If they think you are looking for particular ideas or words it will hamper students' thinking.

Students may ask each other questions, for example, when Examining Similarities and Differences of apples and oranges one may say, "I know that you can cook with apples but can you cook with oranges?" The reply comes from students, not the teacher. If students look to you, the teacher, for the answer direct them back to the group.

In a VESC™ student-centered classroom, the teacher and students ask real questions. Teachers do not ask questions that they know the answers to. If teachers want to find out what students know, they ask them to make a list. Try to keep all questions genuine.

The goals are that students begin to think for themselves and have the skills with which to process academic content independently, and that they are confident and articulate enough to share their thoughts with a group.

General Use of the Skill Steps and the Graphic Organizer Posters

The mental steps of each of the Structured Thinking Skills and the graphic organizers are available as posters for classroom display. Display the posters in the classroom when you are introducing—and whenever students are using—a particular Structured Thinking Skill.

The graphic organizer provides students with a visual way to lay out facts and how they are related. When students are first learning the mental steps required, they should have a copy of the graphic organizer to write on or as a reference. When students have worked with the graphic organizer a number of times they will create their own. This should be encouraged ensuring all the mental steps are incorporated. Students will then better understand that the graphic organizer is a visual representation of the mental steps that we go through when performing the thinking skill. Without understanding the purpose of graphic organizers, students will see them as just another worksheet with blanks to fill in. When the graphic organizer becomes a tool for the expression of their thinking, students will not limited by its format. We do not want students to stop thinking during a step of a skill simply because they run out of room or waste time searching for something to write simply because there is room for more information. Remember we want to push the thinking and learning as far as possible.

INCORPORATING STRUCTURED THINKING SKILLS INTO LESSONS

Once you introduce students to the skill with simple content, they can begin to use the skill with particular curriculum content. You may choose to have them work individually, in pairs, in small groups, or as a whole group for all or some of the steps. Your choice of groupings will depend on the skill you are using and your knowledge of the students. There is further guidance in the following chapters.

1. Start the lesson by having students review the steps of the skill that they are going to use.

2. Present them with the curriculum content and allow them to begin processing.

3. Once they have worked through the skill, they can use the information in a variety of ways. For example, they might write an essay or paragraph, answer a series of questions, or make a chart or draw a diagram explaining what they have learned.

4. Consider creative ways to constantly incorporate the skills into the classroom: For example:

   A. use sentence strips, Post-its®, and index cards for the different steps in a skill, particularly for Supporting a Conclusion, Grouping, and Ordering tasks—they make the ideas tangible and they can be moved around easily.

   B. design classroom centers that highlight the skills.

Mastery of a Skill

It takes time to master a skill fully. Students must use it many times with different content.

**STRUCTURED THINKING SKILL MASTERY WILL
RESULT IN STUDENTS BEING ABLE TO:**

- name the skill and state how they are using it. For example, "I am using the skill of Examining Similarities and Differences to develop my understanding of hurricanes and tornadoes."

- name the mental steps of the skill.

- explain which step they are using.

- attempt every step of the skill.

- explain what their thinking and their summary statement would lack if they skipped any step.

- listen and respond to other group members.

THE VENTURES INITIATIVE AND FOCUS® SYSTEM OF STRUCTURED THINKING

The Ventures Initiative and Focus® System of Structured Thinking lists the different structured thinking skills and strategies as well as methods that can be used to process information. VESC™ selected these skills because of their prevalence in content standards, assessment procedures, curriculum guides, and texts. They are basic to all curriculum areas across grade levels. Students in VESC™ schools utilize a common language of thinking, K-12, develop competence and confidence in the use of these skills, and transfer the skills to other contexts.

During the initial training with VESC™, teachers and students learn the core Structured Thinking Skills: Describing and Defining, Examining Similarities and Differences; Analyzing the Parts of a Whole; Categorizing and Grouping; Ordering by Rank, Time, and Occurrence; and Supporting a Conclusion.

There are four categories of Structured Thinking Skills and Strategies:

- Comprehension Thinking Strategies

- Analytic Thinking Strategies

- Evaluative Thinking Strategies

- Productive Thinking Strategies

THE VENTURES INITIATIVE AND FOCUS®
SYSTEM OF STRUCTURED THINKING

STRUCTURED THINKING STRATEGIES

COMPREHENSION STRATEGIES
Purpose: To understand the significant characteristics of key concepts and to draw interpretations or inferences about them.
- Structured Concept Learning
- Describing and Defining
- Literacy
- Mathematical Thinking
- Informational Literacy
- Academic Preparedness Skills

↕

ANALYTIC THINKING STRATEGIES
Purpose: To understand how significant concepts or processes are interrelated.
- Examining Similarities and Differences
- Analyzing the Parts of a Whole
- Categorizing and Grouping
- Ordering
  - by Time
  - by Occurrence
  - by Rank
- Supporting a Conclusion
  - Examining My Own Conclusion
  - Examining an Author's Conclusion

↕

EVALUATIVE THINKING STRATEGIES
Purpose: To evaluate conclusions or actions based on principles of sound reasoning and reliable information.
- Evaluating Causes
- Evaluating Predictions
- Evaluating Sources of Information
- Evaluating Decisions
- Evaluating Conclusions
  - Conditional Statements
  - Reasons and Assumptions

↕

PRODUCTIVE THINKING STRATEGIES
Purpose: To create original expressions of learned material.
- Generating Ideas
- Creating Analogies and Metaphors
- The Decision-Making Process
  - Decision Framing
  - Analyzing Alternatives
  - Evaluating Alternatives
- Composition Skills
- Problem-Based Learning (PBL)

METHODS

↔

CONSTRUCTIVE COMMUNICATION
- Thinking Aloud Paired Problem Solving
- Visualization
- Effective Group Process
- Assessing Prior Knowledge

↔

STRUCTURED THINKING SKILLS AND PROCESSES
- Making thinking explicit
- Graphic organization of information
- Metacognitive questioning
- Identifying the relation of Structured Thinking Skills to Problem-Based Learning (PBL) and Structured Project Learning (SPL)

COMPREHENSION AND EXPRESSION
- Visualization (rebuilding models)
- Literature Circles
- Author Study
- Comprehension and expression of Structured Thinking
- Structured Project Learning (SPL)

⇩

ACADEMIC ACHIEVEMENT AND EFFECTIVE LIFELONG LEARNING

The first two sections deal with Comprehension and Analytic Thinking Strategies. These are used to develop an understanding of the key characteristics of key concepts and to draw interpretations or inferences about them. The two Structured Thinking Skills that are included in the Comprehension section are Describing and Defining. These skills and the Analytic Thinking Strategies are used to teach content that is new to students. For example, if students are studying the topic of digestion they may start by defining the process digestion. This explanation may be followed by Analyzing the Parts of a Whole of the different organs involved in the digestive system and Ordering by Occurrence what happens to food as the body digests it.

The third section deals with Evaluative Thinking Strategies. These are used to evaluate conclusions or actions based on the principles of sound reasoning and reliable information. In order to make such evaluations, students must have some familiarity with the content. For example, to interpret the action of a character in a novel by Evaluating Decisions, the student must know the story, the character, and the character's actions.

The final section deals with Productive Thinking Strategies are those used to create original expressions of learned material. To do so, students must be very familiar with the content. For example, if we want a student to create metaphor for the process of photosynthesis, he or she must know the skill and have a real understanding of the process of photosynthesis. Without this detailed knowledge, he or she will find it difficult to create an appropriate metaphor.

As the training progresses, you will learn about each of the different strategies including the steps in all the different thinking skills. You will learn how to use the strategies and methods successfully to teach curriculum content. Remember that the Structured Thinking Skills are tools for student mastery of the curriculum.

As stated previously, one can use any skill to clarify any curriculum content. You may find the following flowchart a helpful guide. It helps you think about what students know about the topic and to choose an appropriate skill. Remember that every time students use a skill, even if they know something about the topic, their learning and understanding will deepen by engaging with the content thoughtfully.

FLOWCHART FOR CHOOSING A STRUCTURED THINKING SKILL

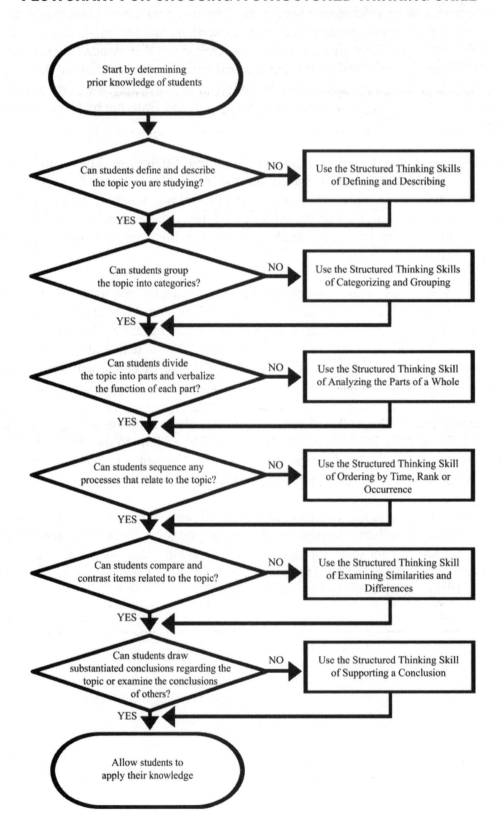

Teacher Self-Check for Coaching and Facilitating Structured Thinking Skills

Use this checklist as a guide to help you teach each Structured Thinking Skill the first time, and then to monitor student progress in using each skill.

INTRODUCING A STRUCTURED THINKING SKILL	
Did I tell students the name of the skill I am going to teach?	
Did I offer a simple explanation of the skill by showing how one uses it in everyday life?	
Did I choose simple material with which to demonstrate the skill the first time so that students can concentrate on the steps without the distraction of difficult material?	
Did I state the steps of the skill clearly?	
Did I explain to the class beforehand that I would not be commenting on or questioning their thinking, but simply writing down what they say? Did I explain that it is the responsibility of their fellow students to question each other's contributions if they are not satisfied with them?	
Did I remind the class of the importance of Effective Group Process in being able to evaluate others' responses?	
Did I facilitate the skill by writing down EXACTLY what they said for each step, without questioning or changing their words?	
Did I refrain from offering "feedback" on their responses, such as saying "good!" to some responses?	
Did I use structures for encouraging them to talk taking into account their ability to communicate with each other? (For example, if my class does not have the Group Process skills to consider constructively and systematically every step of the skill as a large group, did I break them into pairs or small groups, or let them work alone for some of the steps?)	
Did each student take written notes for every step of the skill, recording his or her own thinking and/or class comments?	
Did I ask each student individually to write an interpretation or summary statement of some kind?	
Did I remember throughout the process not to do students' thinking for them, but only to act as a resource for their questions?	

USING A STRUCTURED THINKING SKILL	
Did I tell my students which skill we would be using and remind them of the steps of that skill?	
Did I give them more difficult material this time than I did the first time?	
Did I again remind them to follow the rules of Group Process in discussing their thinking?	
Did I facilitate the steps of the skill without thinking for them, offering comment or praise, or changing their words when I recorded their comments?	
Did I observe any growth in my students' abilities to use this technique and/or communicate their thinking with each other?	
How?	
Next time I use this skill, how may I facilitate it to encourage further growth in my students' ability to use it and to communicate with each other?	

A Student Checklist for Self-Assessment

Students can address the questions on this checklist orally, as they proceed through a skill, or they can answer them in oral or written form after completing the activity. As students become proficient, the checklist may serve as a reminder of what they must do mentally in order to use each skill effectively.

HOW WELL DO I UNDERSTAND AND KNOW HOW TO USE THE STRUCTURED THINKING SKILLS?	
Do I know what thinking skill am I using?	
Can I state how and why am I using this skill right now? (For example, you might say, "I am using the skill of Examining Similarities and Differences to learn about the processes of meiosis and mitosis.")	
Can I state the steps in the skill?	
As I applied each of the steps to the content or information, can I state which step I was using?	
Did I reach a conclusion that allows me to use the original information—to complete a task, answer a question, or write a paper?	
What happened as you went through the mental steps of this skill in applying it to this content? Were any steps in the skill particularly difficult? Why?	

FREQUENTLY ASKED QUESTIONS
ABOUT STRUCTURED THINKING SKILLS

What if my students give wrong information when they are going through the steps of a skill? Should I write it down anyway, or should I correct them?

You should write it down anyway. Teachers should always remind students before beginning work with a skill that, as the class goes through the steps of the skill, the teacher's role is that of facilitator *only*. In that role, the teacher will not comment on, question, or change any students' thinking, unless asked for help. Instead, this responsibility falls on the class. Students must listen carefully to each other and question what they do not understand. Students who offer information are responsible for explaining why they said what they did. If the teacher begins to intervene and "correct" what individuals say, the behavior in the class will not change. You will be back to the usual system in which the four or five students who "know the right answer" always give it, while the others sit passively waiting for information. Once students see that during skills exercises they are truly "allowed" to think aloud without penalty or the fear of being shut down, they will be free to grapple honestly with the material.

The first few times you do skills work, students who have long been passive and simply copied what was on the board may not understand their responsibility to challenge and question each other's ideas. If you trust the process, however, growth will occur. Each time you take students through the steps of the skill, end the exercise by asking them how well they did in terms of Group Process. Did they listen and respond to each other thoughtfully? Ask them to look up at what the teacher recorded on the board and ask if there is anything they see at a second glance that they would like to question. Also, simply be honest with them and tell them that you know they are not used to this kind of "student-centered" thinking, and that it might take time to believe that challenging information is truly up to them alone.

What if I am working with very young children who cannot yet read or write?

All people, no matter what their age, use all of the Structured Thinking Skills without even realizing they are doing so. An infant "compares and contrasts" two toys, and chooses to grab one and reject the other. A toddler sorts treasures found on the playground into different bags, boxes, or hiding places, unconsciously classifying them by his or her criteria. For this reason, you can begin to explain the Structured Thinking Skills and their steps even to preschoolers and they can practice doing them manually, while telling you or a partner what they are doing. You can choose to scribe it on big paper using just letters, or a combination of letters and pictures. You can also ask them to draw what they have just done. For example, a teacher might ask a preschool class to Examine the Similarities and Differences of two kinds of leaves found in the park. As they go through the steps, the teacher might write down what each child says on big paper, large enough for all to see with big letters, in the front of the room. After they have gone through all the steps together, the teacher might ask everyone to say something about the two leaves—a gentle way of asking them to come to a conclusion—then let students call out anything from "I like leaves" to "There are two" to something entirely unrelated. Alternatively, you might ask them all to draw something they learned about these leaves.

How do I know which skill to use with which material?

At the beginning, this will not always be obvious. This is part of your process in understanding what each skill does and why and how to match it to the content you teach. Students must go through this process to become independent users of the skills. After you have practiced each skill a few times, it will be clearer to you which skill is the most appropriate for a given task or content. Most teachers soon realize that they can break down nearly all content using ANY of the skills—it is simply a matter of choosing the one that gets students thinking. One way to know is to plan your lessons by trying several skills with the content you must teach; the best way will probably be the skill that leads most directly to what you want students to know. You might even use two or more skills with the same content. Every time the student uses a skill to engage with the content, his or her understanding will develop. Another way to practice is to take a list of tasks or questions (for example, from the back of a textbook, or from a list of standards for your subject) and matching a skill from the Map of Thinking to each task. This is an excellent way for students to practice fluency with the skills as well.

How do I teach Structured Thinking?

Metacognition is developed.

    A. Students participate in exercises designed to slow down thinking and make them aware of how they think.

    B. To minimize frustration, they proceed at a careful pace, systematically following the sequence of strategies in the Ventures Initiative and Focus® System of Thinking.

Show students how to apply the components of skillful thinking.

    A. Introductory lessons focus on "process" using simple, concrete, familiar, and engaging content.

    B. Students practice the skill through lessons using increasingly complex and abstract content applications.

    C. Teachers design lessons that integrate the thinking skills with the curriculum.

Students learn the skill by having frequent opportunities to work through the process and debrief what they thought and did.

Getting the Meaning: Teaching the Structured Thinking Skill of Defining in the Student-Centered Classroom

*Good teaching is more a giving of right questions
than a giving of right answers.*

—Joseph Albers

GETTING THE MEANING: TEACHING THE STRUCTURED THINKING SKILL OF DEFINING IN THE STUDENT-CENTERED CLASSROOM

6

Defining is the most basic of the Structured Thinking Skills. If we want to define something, we must identify what kind of thing it is and what makes it different from other things of that type. When we encounter something for the first time, we first attempt to place it within a group with which we are already familiar. This is the first step in Defining.

When we define a word, concept, or topic we begin to construct personal meaning and understanding of that word or concept. We cannot build on the meaning and understanding of anything if we are unable to define it. We cannot begin to analyze the parts of a microscope if we do not what a microscope is.

You can clearly define general topics: objects, people, places, or concepts. We usually describe rather than define specific objects, people, places, or things. We define the word "city" but describe the city of New York. We define the office of the president of the United States but describe George Washington. We define "police officer" but describe Officer Patel.

The mental steps in Defining are simple but require the skillful use of language. The frequent use of this skill quickly builds reading level ability.

THE STRUCTURED THINKING SKILL OF DEFINING ENABLES STUDENTS TO:

- construct definitions that have meaning to them personally and build their understanding of the world.

- review terms and concepts in preparation for tests.

- seek clarification when they do not understand something.

- develop vocabulary.

- develop clarity in the use of language.

- develop their reading ability.

TEACHING THE STRUCTURED THINKING SKILL OF DEFINING

In the classroom when students must define a word they usually turn to a glossary or dictionary and copy down whatever appears after the word. If they cannot use a reference, they are often lost as to how to proceed.

Students must be able to construct a definition of a word or concept that has meaning to them personally and one that builds their understanding of the word. Merely copying down or reciting a definition does not bring about understanding and it is quickly forgotten. This skill will enable students to begin to create meaningful definitions.

Introducing the Skill

When first teaching the skill, tell students that are going to learn the Structured Thinking Skill of Defining and ask them to locate it on the chart of the Ventures Initiative and Focus® System of Structured Thinking.

Hold up a picture or an object that is familiar to students. Start with something concrete like an elephant. Have students identify it and say that now they are going to define the object.

 POINTER: **Start simple, concrete, and familiar.**

Do not start with something abstract. This often results in a great deal of debate over the content and students will lose sight of the simple steps in the skill. Once they know it, they can discuss concepts that are more abstract. Try it yourself defining something like "metaphor" or "simile" and you will see that there can be different definitions.

 POINTER: **When to use Defining and when to use Describing.**

Define generic objects, people, places, and concepts; describe particular objects people, places, and concepts. When students must identify a particular thing, they are generally being asked to describe it.

First Step in Skill
Name the large category to which the item belongs.
The first step is to name the large category to which the item belongs. If you ask students to define the word "elephant," the large category could be "mammal" or for young students, "animal."

Second Step in Skill
State enough defining attributes to set the item apart from every other member of the category.

POINTER: Use Effective Group Process or TAPPS techniques.

When teaching and using this skill have, students work in Thinking Aloud Paired Problem Solving pairs or in a group so that they can work together and interact to create definitions and make meaning. Through Effective Group Process, students will work together to create a shared meaning. They will refine their understanding, learn new information, and correct their misunderstandings without ridicule or shutdown. They will learn so much more than they would by looking up a word in a dictionary, though a dictionary or other references may used as resources.

Sample responses for *Elephants*:

Someone may state, "An elephant is a large mammal." Does the characteristic "large" set it apart from every other member of the group or do we need more characteristics? Someone might say that giraffes and bears are large. "An elephant is a large gray mammal." Do the characteristics of "large and gray" set it apart from every other member of the group or do we need more characteristics? Someone might say that a hippopotamus is large and gray. Someone may state, "An elephant is a large gray mammal with a trunk." The group may now be satisfied with the definition. The group or pair works through the process until they are satisfied with the definition.

Third Step in Skill
State a definition.
Ask students to write a definition of the term, for example, "An elephant is a large gray mammal with a trunk." Use Effective Group Process for students to share their definitions. Allow time for students to reflect on the additional information provided by the others and refine their definition if necessary.

 POINTERS

> **Facilitate thinking.**
> The teacher acts as facilitator in this process and does not intervene on the content level. The teacher provides the resource and the type of thinking used and gives students the opportunity to process it.

> **Let students think for themselves.**
> Students must make meaning and ask their own questions. If the teacher intervenes too much, students will think there is a particular answer that the teacher is looking for and they will not try to think through and work things out for themselves. They will just learn by rote the definitions that they believe the teacher wants them to "know" and there will be no real meaning making.

➤ **Learning is more effective using the locale system as opposed to taxon.**
When we learn by memorizing, we process information using the taxon system. This activates only our short-term memory, so what we have learned cannot transfer easily. When we use the Structured Thinking Skill of Defining, we are using the locale system to process the information. Information is more likely to be transferable and go into long-term memory.

➤ **Definitions given will vary.**
Once students have mastered this skill, they will be able to use it to verbalize definitions of terms and phrases that they encounter. For example, the term "triangle" refers to "a shape," "a three-sided shape," "a polygon that has three sides and three angles that total 180°." Students may offer all of the preceding definitions. None of them is wrong. They indicate where the student's thought process or level of understanding is at that time. The responses vary depending on the students' level of understanding.

➤ **Allow students to seek clarification.**
The goal is for students to be able to make meaning from the information whether it is about triangles, a picture book, a number sentence, or a more complex mathematical equation. In an environment in which the communication is constructive, students will be able to seek clarification without threat and mental shutdown. If they think that something is inaccurate, they can ask each other for clarification. By going through this process, students will achieve accuracy and develop understanding regarding the different concepts. Because they have made meaning for themselves, they are far more likely to be able to retain and apply the information.

➤ **Sharing understanding improves communication.**
When we read the definitions outlined previously we may find that they are different from our own. What is important is that we listen and get clarification. A breakdown in communication often occurs when two people are talking about what they think is the same thing but they have a different definition. A breakdown may also occur when two people are talking about the same thing but each gives it a different name. Through Constructive Communication, students can create a shared understanding or definition and learning occurs. Students will develop clarity in their use of terminology and see how a lack of clarity can cause communication difficulties.

As an additional example, use the Structured Thinking Skill of Defining to state who a police officer is.

First Step In Skill
Name the large category to which the item belongs.

Sample responses for a police officer:

The big category could be people who protect us.

Second Step in Skill
State enough defining attributes to set the item apart from every other member of the category.

Someone may state, "Police officers are people who protect us at home." Does this attribute set it apart from every other member of the group or must we add more attributes? Someone might state, "Other people protect us at home." Someone may refine the statement to say, "Police officers are people who work at maintaining order in the neighborhood, town, or city." At this point, the group may be satisfied with the definition.

Third Step in Skill
State the definition.

Police officers are people who work at maintaining order in our towns, cities, and states.

DEFINING

Directions for Elementary Students

Step One: Name the large group to which the item belongs.

Step Two: Give enough attributes to set the item apart from every other member of the group. Ask, "Have I identified enough attributes to set it apart?" "Do other members share these attributes?" If they do, state more.

Step Three: Now state a definition, for example, "A _____ is_____."

DEFINING

Directions for Secondary Students

Step One: Name the large category to which the item belongs.

Step Two: State enough defining attributes to set the item apart from every other member of the category.

Use this question as a check: "Have I identified enough attributes to set it apart from all other members of the group?" If not, state more attributes.

Step Three: State a definition.

INCORPORATING DEFINING INTO LESSONS

You can use this skill with content from all curriculum areas as the main learning activity of a lesson, as a short introductory activity, or as a closing activity.

 POINTERS

> ➤ **Use defining to activate and assess prior knowledge.**
> When embarking on a new topic (e.g., meiosis, odd and even numbers, democracy, etc.), have students verbalize a definition of the topic and categories within it. This will help students connect with the new topic, give you an indication of their level of understanding, and provide a foundation for future learning.

> ➤ **Use defining to review knowledge.**
> This skill can be used to review what has been learned at the end of a lesson or topic (e.g., vocabulary related to the study of volcanoes, communism, or different types of numbers).

SAMPLE DEFINING ACTIVITIES

MATHEMATICS

- whole number
- integer
- real number
- fraction
- addition
- subtraction
- multiplication
- division
- geometry
- trigonometry

ENGLISH LANGUAGE ARTS

- nouns
- main idea
- narrative writing

- expository writing

- persuasive writing

- writing genres

- drama

- comedy

- biography

- poetry

SCIENCE

- hypothesis

- taxonomy

- conclusion

- theory

- solid

- physical change

- chemical change

- element

- compound

- theory of Continental Drift

LEARNING A LANGUAGE
(English Language Learners or Learning a Foreign Language)

- words in different languages

- when to use different verb forms (e.g., *tu* and *vous* in French)

- verbalizing definitions in a different language

- translating words and defining their meaning

SOCIAL STUDIES

- citizen

- worker

- globe
- map
- culture
- honesty
- deception
- hopes
- family
- philosophy

PHYSICAL EDUCATION

- balance
- exercise
- teamwork
- basketball, volleyball, or golf
- competition

THE ARTS

- theater
- orchestra
- impressionism
- choreography
- different musical notes

TECHNOLOGY

- computer, mouse, keyboard
- Internet
- video player
- digital camera
- different methods of communication

Painting a Picture: Teaching the Structured Thinking Skill of Describing in the Student-Centered Classroom

*The job of an educator is to teach students
to see the vitality in themselves.*

—Joseph Campbell

We are all familiar with directions such as "Describe a … (topic)." Parents, children, and professionals in every area use the skill in interactions with each other. We find these directions in daily classroom activities. Of course, everyone uses the skill daily to communicate information to others. Sometimes we do it well and sometimes it is the basis for confusion. The systematic teaching of the mental steps in the Structured Thinking Skill of Describing helps avoid this confusion.

DESCRIBING AND DEFINING

Students often find it hard to differentiate between a definition and a description of an item. As they learn the different Structured Thinking Skills, students realize that each skill has particular mental steps. As we teach the steps in each skill explicitly to students, they develop a confidence toward learning and a greater understanding of the content information.

We usually ask students to define an item or a concept before we ask them to describe it. The differences in a definition of an item and a description of an item should be clear in the mind of students before they proceed.

- A *definition* of an item will include the large group to which the item belongs plus the characteristics of the item that set it apart from all the other members of the group. A definition of an item does *not* include *all* the characteristics of the items in the group. It only includes the characteristics of the item that *set it apart* from everything else in the group. The definition of an item assumes that the listener or the reader already knows the general characteristics of the group to which the item belongs. Whether or not this assumption is accurate is determined during the discussion that follows.

- A *description* of the item will include *all* the attributes of the item that we could use to draw a clear picture in the mind of someone else. Students must first define these attributes and then choose terminology that adequately expresses them.

Consider these differences related to the word giraffe:

Definition: A giraffe is an animal that is at least ten feet tall, has a long neck, and is yellow with brown spots.

Description: In order to describe a giraffe, I will use the physical characteristics of size, shape, color, and texture of covering. I will use the classification characteristics of kingdom, phylum, class, order, family, genus, and species. (Factual information for each characteristic is then compiled and communicated.)

It is important to remember that a definition of an item will have no meaning to the student if the student does not have a mental picture of the item formed by the words used in the definition. Therefore, the mental skills of Defining and Describing go hand-in-hand to build meaning and understanding for the student.

THE STRUCTURED THINKING SKILL OF DESCRIBING ENABLES STUDENTS TO:

- independently construct a description of an object or concept.

- move away from processing information by rote memorization.

- develop verbal communication skills.

- develop a clear mental picture of the object or concept.

- retain information developed during the construction of the description.

- increase reading comprehension levels.

- increase performance levels on standardized tests.

- build confidence and self-esteem.

- write more effectively.

TEACHING THE STRUCTURED THINKING SKILL OF DESCRIBING

The reason that student responses vary so much when asked to describe an item or a concept is that we have not taught them the specific steps in the skill. Students who learn to describe objects or concepts, ideas, and issues well use the skill throughout their life.

Introducing the Skill
When first teaching the skill, tell students that are going to learn the Structured Thinking Skill of Describing and ask them to locate it on the Ventures Initiative and Focus® System of Structured Thinking. First, introduce the skill with an object that students can describe. Introduce description of concepts, ideas, or issues after the steps of a description of an object are familiar to students.

First Step in Skill
State the purpose of the description, i.e., humor, explanation, insight, inspiration, or aesthetic.
The purpose of the description may be included in the task that students must complete or they may state it for themselves. Possible purposes include humor, explanation, to gain

insight, to provide insight, or purely aesthetic. When teaching the skill, choose an example that is familiar to students. In this example, students are describing the English Setter breed of dog.

Sample response:

> I am describing an English Setter to gain insight into the characteristics and needs of this breed of dog.

Second Step In Skill
Create a mental picture of the item.
It is very hard to try to describe an object that you cannot visualize. Students should have a beginning mental picture of the object they are attempting to describe. Provide students with photographs of English Setters.

Third Step In Skill
Verbalize the attributes of each item: size, shape, color, texture, smell, sound, etc.
Ask students to verbalize the attributes of the object they are describing. Say that they are to assume the listener has no idea what the object might be. The attributes will depend on the object but may include size, shape, color, texture, etc.

Sample responses for a dog may include:

> Color and pattern
> Size
> Shape
> Breed
> Sex
> Age
> Sound of the bark

Allow students to choose attributes that will describe the object accurately. They may add to the list or delete attributes they consider inappropriate.

A fun exercise is to have students choose an item to describe to the class without telling anyone what the item is. A student gives a verbal description of the item and each classmate determines what it is. The student describing the item can assess whether or not the description was accurate by the responses from his or her classmates. If everyone responds by identifying the same object, then the description was accurate. If classmates respond by identifying different objects from the one described, then the description was not accurate.

Fourth Step in Skill

Verbalize how each attribute is significant, using analogies or making connections with prior knowledge.

Ask students to consider each attribute and explain how it is significant. Use Effective Group Process to share different ideas. This will help students determine what words and phrases build clear pictures in the minds of a listener or reader. Students will see that they may have different ideas than other members of the group. As they participate, they will develop their understanding of the term.

 POINTER: What do we mean by significance?

> When you first teach this skill, students may not have developed a mental model for the term significances. You may need to clarify this before or if it is an issue at this step of the skill.

Sample response:

Attribute	Significance	Connection/Analogies
Color and pattern	Certain breeds are particular colors.	Dalmatians are black and white. Labradors are black or gold.
Size	Is it a large, small, or medium sized breed?	Dogs very greatly in size from the small Chihuahua to the enormous Great Dane.
Shape	Certain breeds have a distinctive shape.	The sausage dog or daschund, head of a German shepherd.
Breed	There are many different breeds. Some pedigree dogs are very valuable. Certain breeds are good for particular tasks.	Part of the setter group of breeds, e.g., Irish Setter, Gordon Setter.
Sex	Females capable of having pups.	If you were buying a dog, you may want to breed pups.
Age	Is it a puppy or adult dog? They behave quite differently.	Puppies are very playful but need training and may cause damage.
Sound of the bark	Does the dog have a distinctive bark? Does it bark a lot?	Some breeds of dog bark a lot.
Temperament	Gentle, mild mannered, good with children	The breed may make a good family pet.
Use	Gun dog	Gun dogs are used for hunting.

POINTER: **When to use Defining and when to use Describing**

> We define generic objects, people, places, and concepts. We describe particular objects people, places, and concepts. When we ask students to identify a particular thing, we are generally asking them to describe it.

During this step, students are really making meaning of the information. They relate the information to what they already know and make analogies that may be very simple or more complex.

Students can integrate this step of the skill with writing for a particular audience. Students should have some knowledge of the prior knowledge of the audience to communicate effectively with them. Students often assume that others have similar background experiences and are surprised to learn that not everyone has seen the same movies, watched the same television shows, traveled to the same places, or played the same sports. In the descriptions students develop, they often use phrases such as "a goliath," "of dinosaur proportions," "intergalactic travel." If others question them regarding the meanings of these phrases they will realize that they must pay particular attention to the words used in their descriptions.

 POINTER: **Different people have different ideas of the same word**

> Students are surprised to learn that "What I say" and "What people hear" can be very different. Literacy skills become vital in organizing information in all inquiries in the classroom as well as in broader settings. For example, a student may describe the color of a dog as brown when the student's mental image is tan. The listener may perceive the dog as being a very dark color. The person describing the animal will realize that the description is inaccurate if they use the single word, brown to describe the dog's color.

Fifth Step In Skill
Add details by developing words and phrases that accurately communicate your mental picture to others.
Ask students to consider each attribute and identify the characteristics for the item that they are describing. During this step of the skill, students add new vocabulary words to their language development. They realize that words are necessary for accurate communication of information. As they work, they may add or remove attributes.

Sample response:

Attribute	Words/Phrases
Color and pattern	White flecked with black
Size	Medium-sized dog, 20-25 inches tall, 60-65 lbs.
Shape	Clean outline, long ears, squarish head, short straight tail
Breed	English Setter
Sex	Female
Age	Adult dog
Sound of the bark	Does the dog have a distinctive bark? Does it bark a lot?
Temperament	Gentle, mild mannered, good with children
Use	Gun dog

Sixth Step in Skill
Restate or read your description to check for accuracy.
As students read the description aloud, they often find that the description they hear is not accurate enough. They must have the opportunity to modify the original description, and make sure that the words accurately describe their mental image.

Sample response before modification:

> This dog is an English setter that is quite large and has long, white hair with black flecks. It has a small straight tail. It is female, and can have many puppies.

Modifications might include:

> height in feet and inches.
>
> weight in pounds.
>
> sex determination for all English setters.
>
> tail length relative to body size of animal.
>
> comments about temperament and use.

Students can modify their descriptions as many times as necessary until satisfied that the description accurately depicts the object.

DESCRIBING A PIECE OF MUSIC

Purpose: To describe a piece of classical music, Eine Kleine Nachtmusik, to explore its structure and style.		
Mental picture:		

Attribute	Significance	Connection/Analogy
Title	To know what the piece is called. Does it have a title that is in words	Many titles have a common name they are know by e.g. Beethoven's Ninth Symphony is known as the Choral Symphony
Composer	Who wrote the music? Is it someone well known?	Famous classical composers include Mozart, Bach, Beethoven
Style	Is it pop, classical, music of a particular type?	I like pop music.
Movements	The structure of the piece	Classical music is often broken into sections.
Tempo	The tempo varies in many pieces.	Do you dance to it? Is it fast or slow?
Musical Instruments	Is it a piece written for a full orchestra, chamber orchestra, or solo instrument?	Can the piece be played on just one or a few instruments or is something really lost by this.
Composed/ performed?	How old is the piece?	

Develop words/phrases that accurately communicate your mental picture	
Attribute	**Words and Phrases**
Title	Eine Kleine Nachtmusik (Mozart's quick description); Serenade in G Major
Composer	Wolfgang Amadeus Mozart
Style	Classical nocturne
Movements	When first performed was a five-movement work. • Allegro Minuet and Trio • Romance Minuet and Trio • Finale Now consists of three movements. • Romance Minuet and Trio • Finale
Musical Instruments	Played as an orchestral piece or by five solo strings. There is ambiguity over Mozart's intention
Composed/ performed?	Eighteenth century. First performed in Vienna, August 10th 1787.

Description: Mozart composed Eine Kleine Nachtmusik. It was first performed in Vienna in 1787. Although originally longer, it now consists of three movements. Either a full orchestra or a quintet can play it.

DESCRIBING A TRIANGLE

Purpose: To describe a triangle to examine its structure		
Mental picture: 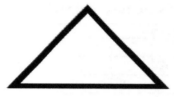		
Attribute	**Significance**	**Analogy or connection with what I know**
Number of sides	Tells you the category of shape it belongs to	Tripods, tricycle, triceratops, three bears
Length of sides	Tells you whether it is an equilateral shape	Balanced, the same
Number of angles	Particular shapes have a particular number of angles	Three corners
Size/type of angles	Tells you a particular type of shape	In a triangle the angles add up to 180 degrees
Develop words/phrases that accurately communicate your mental picture		
Attribute	**Words and phrases**	
Number of sides	three	
Length of sides	equal	
Number of angles	three	
Size/type of angles	sixty degrees, acute angles	
Description: This is an equilateral triangle. It has three sides of equal length. They are one inch long. Each of the angles is sixty degrees.		

DESCRIBING AN ATOM

Purpose: To describe an atom to gain insight into its structure		
Mental picture:		

Attribute	**Significance**	**Analogy or connection with what I know**
Size	How big or small do I make it? Can I see just one atom?	A picture of a person is not the person, but I can blow up a picture to make it larger, and see it better
Shape	Are they round, square, rectangular, or triangular?	The shape of the atom is determined by a "picture" that is blown up; and sometimes the shape of the atom changes as the electrons move within the electron cloud
Color	Do they all have one color, or are they different colors?	A handful of sulfur is yellow, but a handful of silver is not
Parts	If an atom is too small to see, how can it possibly have parts?	The protons and the neutrons are in the nucleus and are about the same size; the electrons are supposedly so small they are almost no there

Develop words/phrases that accurately communicate your mental picture	
Attribute	**Words and phrases**
Size	So small that they can hardly be seen with the most powerful microscopes
Shape	The present shape is thought to be a dense center with spirals around it
Color	Some atoms have color and some atoms have no color
Parts	The basic parts are protons, neutrons, and electrons and there are also some other parts, but they are not in our book

Description: An atom is a very tiny particle that has a small nucleus. The protons and the neutrons are packed together in the small nucleus. The electrons are tiny particles that "swarm" around the nucleus. The model of the atom in the book shows that the electrons are in circular orbits around the nucleus. The picture on the front of the book shows orbits that are not circles. The orbits are oblong, and look like figure eights with the nucleus as the center point.

DESCRIBING

<u>**Directions for Elementary Students**</u>

Step One: Close your eyes and try to see the thing that you are describing.

Step Two: Think about the different aspects of the thing that you are going to describe: size, shape, color, texture, smell, sound, etc.

Step Three: Use each of the aspects to describe the object.

Step Four: Read your description to your classmates. Do they know what you are describing?

DESCRIBING

<u>**Directions for Secondary Students**</u>

Step One: State the purpose of the description, i.e., humor, explanation, insight, inspiration, or aesthetic.

Step Two: Create a mental picture of the item.

Step Three: Verbalize the attributes of each item: size, shape, color, texture, smell, sound, etc.

Step Four: Verbalize how each attribute is significant, using analogies or making connections with prior knowledge.

Step Five: Add details by developing words and phrases that accurately communicate your mental picture to others.

Step Six: Restate or read your description to check for accuracy.

INCORPORATING THE STRUCTURED THINKING SKILL OF DESCRIBING INTO LESSONS

Students can use this skill to describe objects, concepts, ideas, or issues in every curriculum area. We often ask students to describe something without teaching them these simple steps. When introducing new content to students, the skills of Definition and Description are an excellent place to start. First take students through an exercise where they define the concept or object, then have them write a description of the term. Both of these exercises will help them begin to construct meaning. They can then apply other Structured Thinking Skills to develop their understanding.

They can use the Structured Thinking Skills of Defining and Describing again at the end of a unit to make a comparison with their definitions and descriptions written at the beginning. They will gain insight into how their understanding has developed.

SAMPLE DESCRIBING ACTIVITIES

ENGLISH LANGUAGE ARTS

- a humorous description of a character in a story
- the plot of a screenplay
- a war hero to show his or her bravery
- a satirical description of current events
- the life of a writer
- the setting for a scary story
- a classmate: can the rest of the class figure out who it is?
- your town in a way demonstrates its history
- your favorite film or recording artist
- a mouthwatering meal

MATHEMATICS

- shapes in terms of their properties
- a right triangle
- a graph or chart to explain the information that it shows
- the relationship between figures
- different properties of a number
- rational numbers
- area in the terms of its dimensions, weight, volume, etc.
- measurement systems
- number patterns

SCIENCE

- chemical change
- the Solar System
- animal cells
- the human heart
- different states of matter
- a compound
- an element's atomic structure
- the structure of a flower
- cloning
- a particular food web or chain

SOCIAL STUDIES

- a country in terms of its economy
- The Crusades
- the Mexican Revolution
- New York City
- great individuals in history
- land formations
- costume or fashion in a particular period in history
- early forms of transport
- The Wall Street Crash
- America's involvement in the Second World War

LEARNING A LANGUAGE
(English Language Learners or Learning a Foreign Language)

- a person or object in the different language
- different aspects of the culture (e.g., music, the home)
- significant historical events in the country concerned
- significant individuals from the past or present in the country concerned

PHYSICAL EDUCATION

- how to play a particular game
- exercise
- muscle groups
- basketball
- teamwork

THE ARTS

- a particular painting or piece of music
- characters in a play
- a painting technique
- the life of an artist or musician
- comedy

TECHNOLOGY

- computer
- a particular web site
- a DVD player
- computer applications
- server

FREQUENTLY ASKED QUESTIONS ABOUT DEFINING AND DESCRIBING

Why do my students have difficulty determining the group to which the item belongs when they are developing a definition for a word?

Students usually are looking to the teacher to provide the "right answer" to the "blank." Teachers understand this behavior. Explain to students that it is acceptable to put the word into any group that they think is appropriate. Assure them that they can place an item in any one of several groups and that all the groups are accurate representations of the item. It will take several weeks of reinforcing this idea for students to become comfortable initiating responses based on their own thinking.

My students cannot determine the differences in a definition and a description. How do I explain this?

A definition of an item assumes that the audience has some understanding of the group to which the item belongs. It also assumes that the audience has some understanding of the members of the group. A description of an item does not make this assumption. A description of an item includes every aspect of the item that the individual can perceive, and then relates this information to the audience. A description is more complete than a definition.

My students do not know how to describe an item adequately. They want to state one aspect of the item and call it a description. How do I get them to write more in-depth descriptions?

Ask students create mental models of the description BEFORE they write. The mental model of a description of a football might include such aspects as size, shape, material it is made of, game it is used in, price, and life expectancy. The mental model of a description of George Washington would include different aspects: place of birth, country he lived in, education, profession, accomplishments, and significance of his efforts to the country. The descriptions students write will be more effective if they first create these mental models.

My students think that the way to "define" a word is to copy the word from the glossary of the reference or from the dictionary. How do I break this habit?

Explain to students that they are going to learn to define a word using their own language abilities to create the definition. Use a list of items students know to practice the manipulation of language in creating an accurate definition. Begin with a word such as "giraffe." Students will probably place the word in the group "animal." Then they will give one other characteristic of the giraffe that is outstanding in their mental picture of a giraffe. An example might be, "A giraffe is an animal that is very tall." The next step is very important to students' understanding: ask them to assess each definition to determine whether the definition sets the item apart from everything else in the group. Have students ask the questions, "Does this definition set the animal apart from every other animal?" and "Are there any other tall animals?" The questions will quickly demonstrate to students that they use language to communicate accurately specific information. Reading levels can change simply from students learning how to define and describe different words accurately.

It's All Apples and Oranges: Teaching the Structured Thinking Skill of Examining Similarities and Differences in the Student-Centered Classroom

Memorization is what we resort to when what we are learning makes no sense.

—Anonymous

IT'S ALL APPLES AND ORANGES: TEACHING THE STRUCTURED THINKING SKILL OF EXAMINING SIMILARITIES AND DIFFERENCES IN THE STUDENT-CENTERED CLASSROOM

8

We continually look at things in terms of how they are similar and how they are different. We use the significance of similarities and differences to make choices between things or gain insight. For example:

When buying a new winter coat, you may have narrowed the selections to two choices.

Both coats are thick, warm, long, and comfortable. They have pockets for convenience, must be dry-cleaned, and are about the same price.

You then look at how they are different.

One is off-white and one is dark brown: the cream one would show the dirt and require more dry cleaning, making it costly and inconvenient The brown coat fastens with a zipper, which may break, while the off-white coat has buttons, which may fall off: you must consider how well you can have fasteners repaired or replaced. The brown coat has a hood and the cream one has a collar: you must decide whether you will use the hood or whether you commonly wear a hat.

Because of maintenance and convenience, you select the brown coat.

You used Examining Similarities and Differences to help you choose, but you did it naturally, without recognizing your thinking as you were choosing the coat.

EXAMINING SIMILARITIES AND DIFFERENCES
ENABLES STUDENTS TO:

- make carefully considered choices between two or more items.

- develop an understanding of the subtle differences between two similar things or ideas in order to differentiate them.

- conceptualize or clarify two abstract or complex ideas.

- respond to questions on standardized tests in which they are required to compare and contrast, or examine similarities and differences.

- meet the state standards that require compare and contrast.

- develop reading comprehension by sustaining particular focus while reading.

- produce a well-structured piece of writing in any curriculum area. Students use the notes taken while using the skill to organize their writing.

- review concepts prior to testing.

TEACHING THE STRUCTURED THINKING SKILL OF EXAMINING SIMILARITIES AND DIFFERENCES

When teaching any Structured Thinking Skill for the first time, start with very simple content so that students can focus on the process. For Examining Similarities and Differences, start with something concrete and familiar such as an apple and an orange.

Introducing the Skill

Tell students that they are going to learn the Structured Thinking Skill of Examining Similarities and Differences and have them locate it on the Ventures Initiative and Focus® System of Thinking. Ask them for examples where they have been asked to think about things in terms of their similarities and differences. Student responses might include compare and contrast questions on exams, identifying likenesses or similarities of two or more objects, and identifying the differences between two or more things. Ask them to discuss what they thought about when completing such tasks or assignments. Say that they will be learning the Structured Thinking Skill of Examining Similarities and Differences which will allow them to complete these assignments in a comprehensive and systematic way.

First Step in Skill
Identify the two things you are examining.
Hold up the two things and ask students to state what they are. Write the names of the two items on the chalkboard or chart paper as shown:

Sample response:

First Item	Second Item
Apple	Orange

Second Step In Skill

Identify similarities between the two things, the attribute of each similarity, and how each similarity is significant.

Ask the students to list all the similarities that they can think of between the two things. Ask them to identify the attribute of similarity. Say that similarities are the ways that the two things are alike. Have the students explain how each similarity is significant.

Sample responses may include:

Attribute	Similarity	Significance
Part of plant	They are both fruits.	Both are part of the plant that we eat. Fruits are usually sweet.
Shape	They are round.	Most fruits are round. The flesh protects the seeds encased inside the fruit.
Where they grow	They grow on trees.	Method of cultivation
Edibility	You can eat them.	They are nutritious.
Usability	You can cook with them or eat them raw.	You can eat them on their own or as an ingredient in other food products.

Get as many ideas from students as you can.

 Pointers:

> **Write all answers verbatim and avoid shutdown.**
> Write down exactly what students say. Remember at this stage that you want the students to think about every aspect of the two objects and explain their thinking. If you begin to change or paraphrase what they say, some students may shut down, thinking that they do not know what you want. Others may not share their thinking, giving only responses that they think you want to hear if they think that you looking for particular ideas or words.

> **Allow questioning among students.**
> Students may ask each other questions, for example, "I know that you can cook with apples but can you cook with oranges?" Another student might reply, "Oranges are cooked to make marmalade." You want students to respond to each other. If students look to you for the answer, direct them back to the group. Tell students to seek clarification of comments that they do not understand or they think is wrong. Of course, they should seek clarification in a way that maintains constructive communication.

Third Step in Skill
Identify the differences between the two things, the attribute of each difference, and explain how each difference is significant.

Ask students to list all the differences between the two things. As they state differences, they should identify the attribute of each difference and explain how each difference is significant.

Organize responses as follows:

Attribute	First Item	Second Item	Significance
Color	Are green or red	Orange	Identification
Climate	Grows in temperate climate	Grows in warmer climates	Cultivation
Structure	The flesh is one unit	Has segments	Way that the fruit can be broken apart.
Edibility of the peel	You can eat the peel	The pith part is very bitter	Have to peel away the part that is indigestible or disagreeable.

 Pointers:

> **Have references available.**
> Students will have many ideas and may raise questions that require factual answers. For example, they may need to find out in what sort of climate oranges grow. It may be useful to have resources about apples and oranges available.

> **Accept all responses.**
> If students give attributes that you do not agree with, just write them down. Remember that you want students to think for themselves. As they get more experienced, their attributes will become more precise.

> **Have students express complete thoughts.**
> When they are listing the differences students need to explain their thinking. Do not accept one-word contributions like "orange" or "green." Students need to explain the whole thought. For example, "Apples are green or red and oranges are orange. The attribute is color." "My attribute is the color of the seeds. Orange seeds are white and apple seeds are brown." This helps students learn to become more descriptive, succinct, and focused in their thinking and communication. Tell students that they may write down additional similarities and differences presented by other students if they want to include them in their work.

> ➤ **Ask students to explain their choices.**
> One student may have something listed as a similarity and another as a difference. As students explain why they placed something where they did, they may uncover attributes that are more discriminating. For example, one student may have the fact that they are both fruit as a likeness and another may have fruit as the category and the orange listed as a citrus fruit and the apple as a rosaceous fruit. Dialogue between two students results in richer learning for them, their classmates, and their teacher.

Fourth Step In Skill

Use the similarities, differences, and their significance to state an interpretation or summary regarding the two objects.

Ask students to examine the similarities, differences, and significance to write their summary statements. Initially students may be reluctant to do this and their summary statements may be quite simplistic. As students become more experienced, they will write summary statements that are more meaningful.

Sample response:

> While apples and oranges are both sweet, edible fruits that grow on trees, they grow in different climates. Apples grow best in a temperate climate while oranges need a subtropical climate.

 POINTERS

> ➤ **Discuss mental tension.**
> During this step, students really have to draw inferences, creating some mental tension. Talk to them about this. This feeling is natural.

> ➤ **Show that there are many valid summary statements.**
> When students first Examine Similarities and Differences they often think that there is one specific summary statement. The quickest way to dispel this idea is to ask students to share all their ideas and explore the variation and depth of responses.

> ➤ **Encourage students to share their summary statements.**
> Initially each student should read his or her summary statement to the whole group. Thank students for their contributions. As students become more experienced, they may just read it to a partner or smaller group. In the initial stages of learning the skill, students benefit from hearing a wide range of summary statements both in form and in content.
>
> After this, allow students some time to refine their summary statements and make sure that their notes are clear so they are able to write them up. There is no set way of refining the summary statements. They may want to incorporate something they heard into their summary statement or, having said it aloud, alter it in some way.

EXAMINING SIMILARITIES AND DIFFERENCES

Directions for Primary and Elementary Students

Step One: You are going to examine the similarities and differences between two things. What are they called?

Step Two: Can you say some of the ways that they are alike? When you state a way they are alike, give the attribute. For example, if I say that they are both round, the attribute is shape.

Step Three: Can you say some of the ways that they are different? When you state a difference, give the attribute. For example, if I say that this is blue and this is yellow, the attribute is color.

Step Four: Now look at all of the information. Decide what is important and say a few sentences about the two things that you have compared and contrasted.

EXAMINING SIMILARITIES AND DIFFERENCES

Directions for Secondary Students

Step One: Identify the two things you are examining.

Step Two: Identify similarities between the two things, the attribute of each similarity, and how each similarity is significant. For example, if I say that they are both round, the attribute is shape.

Step Three: Identify the differences between the two things, the attribute of each difference, and explain how each difference is significant. For example, if I say that this is blue and this is yellow, the attribute is color.

Step Four: Use the similarities, differences, and their significance to state an interpretation or summary regarding the two things.

INCORPORATING EXAMINING SIMILARITIES
AND DIFFERENCES INTO LESSONS

The Structured Thinking Skill of Examining Similarities and Differences is often needed to meet both state standards and testing requirements. The whole skill or parts of it can be used anytime that students are required to compare and contrast or think about likenesses and differences. In English Language Arts classes students are often asked to analyze texts or characters by comparing and contrasting them. In mathematics, examining similarities and differences helps students clarify and remember abstract concepts, such as real and imaginary numbers. In geometry, recognizing similarity and congruence requires the examination of similarities and differences between figures. In science, students may be asked to compare and contrast organisms that have resulted from convergent evolution, to differentiate living things, or understand the properties of different states of matter. In history, students may be asked to reflect on the differences between societies separated by time. This skill can be used to complete these assignments or tasks.

SAMPLE EXAMINING SIMILARITIES AND DIFFERENCES ACTIVITIES

MATHEMATICS

- two polygons

- concepts of area and perimeter

- mean, median, and mode

- measurement systems

- two graphs or lines on a graph

- different number systems

- real and imaginary numbers

- rational and irrational numbers

- formulas for pyramids and cones

- greatest common factor and least common multiple

ENGLISH LANGUAGE ARTS

- two stories by the same author

- two poems

- different versions of the same story

- a wolf as depicted in two different stories

- two characters
- two literary devices (e.g., metaphor and simile)
- different genres of writing
- different writing on the same theme or idea
- a book vs. the movie version of the book
- a character at the beginning and end of a novel

SOCIAL STUDIES

- jobs (e.g., police officer and firefighter)
- aspects of life today and in the past
- a map and a globe
- ancient and modern civilizations to understand their contributions
- kinds of political or economic systems
- religious or cultural beliefs
- everyday life in different cultures
- primary and secondary earthquake waves
- leaders
- goods and services
- revolutions, movements, war and terrorism

SCIENCE

- summer and winter; spring and fall
- liquid water and frozen water
- animal cells and plant cells
- different body systems
- different forces (e.g., electricity and magnetism)
- different molecular structures
- ecosystems
- kinds of energy
- weight and mass
- force and work

LEARNING A LANGUAGE

(English Language Learners or Learning a Foreign Language)

- familiar words in two languages (e.g., hello and goodbye)
- words in different languages
- structure of the same sentence in different languages
- aspects of life in the different countries (e.g., school, economy, music)
- use of subjunctive

PHYSICAL EDUCATION

- clothing worn for PE and for everyday
- team and individual sports
- the rules of different sports
- different gymnastic movements
- different types of dance, dance steps, etc.
- types of exercise for health benefits
- nutritional value of foods
- physical condition of smoker vs. nonsmoker

THE ARTS

- painting of an object and photograph of an object
- paintings by the same artist
- different portrait, landscape, or still life paintings
- two bars of music
- treble and bass staves
- two musical instruments
- two versions of the same song or pieces of music
- different periods of painting, dance, etc.
- styles of architecture
- the print and film version of a book

TECHNOLOGY

- laptop and desktop computer

- different search engines

- different Web sites

- digital camera and traditional camera

- hard drives and removable media drives on a computer

- floppy disks and burnable CDs

- computer printing vs. photocopying to produce multiple copies

- Internet and Intranet

- email and regular mail

- electronic and hard copy

FREQUENTLY ASKED QUESTIONS ABOUT EXAMINING SIMILARITIES AND DIFFERENCES

My students write a conclusion that is unrelated to any of the ways the items are alike or different. What do I do?

Students do not yet understand that the mental steps in the skill are connected. They are still responding to each part of the graphic organizer as a fill-in-the-blank exercise. Ask students to state a conclusion based on how they are alike or how they are different. You can also have students state the purpose of examining similarities and differences.

My students write a conclusion that is a restatement of one of the ways the items are alike or different. What do I do?

Allow this initially. It is a natural step in learning to use the steps in the mental skill to develop meaning and understanding. They will expand their comprehension as they use the skill to organize information that is more complex.

The Cog and the Wheel: Teaching the Structured Thinking Skill of Analyzing the Parts of a Whole in the Student-Centered Classroom

Information cannot replace education.

—Imparato and Itarari

THE COG AND THE WHEEL: TEACHING THE STRUCTURED THINKING SKILL OF ANALYZING THE PARTS OF A WHOLE IN THE STUDENT-CENTERED CLASSROOM

9

When we try to make sense of something, we often break the subject down into its integral parts. Then we consider how these parts fit together to form the whole. For example, when we have a new digital camera or food processor, we first inspect the different parts. We may ask what a gadget or button does and what is its relationship to the operation of the whole object.

This skill enables us to examine things ranging from the very simple to the complex. To describe a film we may mention the actors, the plot, the cinematography, the soundtrack, and so on. As well as analyzing physical things, we also break down processes, concepts, or the elements that contribute to a whole.

You can apply this Structured Thinking Skill to content and skills. Students use this skill to process curriculum content about complex mechanisms or systems, for example, to Analyze the Parts of a Whole of the endocrine system or a calculator. Students learn to identify the components of a well-written report or interpreting graphs, charts, and tables.

ANALYZING THE PARTS OF A WHOLE ENABLES STUDENTS TO:

- break down and understand the function of a large system or object.

- analyze charts and graphs.

- analyze a prose passage, either fact or fiction, for basic comprehension or to write a response.

- develop vocabulary. Students say "Now what do we call that part?" when identifying the component parts of an object.

- deepen their knowledge and understanding of the objects, theories, and concepts in a systematic way, rather than rote memorization or partial conceptualization.

- deepen their knowledge and understanding of plays, films, novels, or other texts.

TEACHING THE STRUCTURED THINKING SKILL OF ANALYZING THE PARTS OF A WHOLE

As with all the Structured Thinking Skills, explain the process and purpose using something simple so that students can focus on learning the steps. Introduce Analyzing the Parts of a Whole with a familiar object without too many parts. Use the actual artifact in a demonstration—a teapot, a pair of scissors, or a clock work well. You may also use something relevant to a particular curriculum area (e.g., a calculator, paintbrush, football, compass, etc.).

Introducing the Skill

When introducing the skill, tell students that they are going to learn a new Structured Thinking Skill called Analyzing the Parts of a Whole and ask them to locate the skill on the Ventures Initiative and Focus® System of Structured Thinking.

First Step in Skill

Identify the whole object.

Ask students to identify the whole object. The example that follows considers a pair of scissors.

Second Step in Skill

Identify the parts of the whole.

Have students list the different parts. See the sample response that identifies the parts of a pair of scissors. Students may respond differently.

Sample response:

> The whole is a pair of scissors. The parts include the blades, the handles, and the nut and bolt.

 POINTER: **Accept all responses.**

> Sometimes students will list things that you may not consider physical parts of an item, such as color or texture. Just record them and go through the process with everything that students list. As they become more experienced in their thinking, they will become more selective in the parts that they list. Remember to let go! Students will learn to distinguish between attributes and the parts of something as they become more experienced. The Structured Thinking Skills of Definition and Description will also help develop their understanding.

Third Step in Skill

For each part, identify the function and what would happen if the part were not there.

Now examine each part in turn and have students explain its function and what would happen if that part were not there. Students complete this step in two parts. Depending on the content, students may first explain the function and next what would happen if the part were not there. The order does not matter as long as both parts of the steps are completed.

Record student responses regarding each of the parts. For example, if the blades were not there, there would be nothing to cut with; therefore the function of the blade is to provide a cutting edge.

Continue analyzing each part with students. If the screw were not there, the blades would not hold together. They would not be able to slide in order to cut. Therefore, the function of the blades is to hold the two blades together so that they can slide and work as a pair of scissors.

If the handles were not there, it would be very difficult to hold scissors and move the blades. Therefore, the function of the handle is to provide an easy way of gripping the scissors.

 POINTERS

> **Tell students to "Give it a try!"**
> This step pushed students' thinking. Students may say things like "I don't get it." "What do you mean?" State the question again referring to a particular part. For example, "What would happen if the blades were not there?"

> **Focus on making meaning.**
> A text will often describe the function of something and when reading it a student can just pull out or copy this piece of information. For example, a text on flowers may state, "The function of the petal is to attract insects." Students can write this down without having to think about the information. If they have to answer the question, "What would happen if this part were not there?" they have to mentally process that piece of information. They have to create meaning. They may bring in what they know, beyond what the text states.

Fourth Step in Skill
Use all the information to state an interpretation or summary to describe how the parts contribute to the whole.
Ask students to write a summary statement or interpretation regarding the whole object and its parts.

Sample response:

> A pair of scissors is a portable object that you can use to cut paper and other material. It is made of two blades that slide together to cut.

 POINTERS

> **Accept students' thoughts and comments as they are.**
> Students may find this stage difficult. Their summary statements may be simple. A common response early on is "A pair of scissors" (or whatever the whole is) "is more than the sum of its parts." As with all the skills, as students become more experienced their summary statements will become more sophisticated.

➤ **Use a variety of student groupings.**
Students can work at each of the stages of the skill individually, in pairs, or as a large group.

➤ **Allow students to record responses in different ways.**
Very young children and students with writing difficulties can record their responses in the form of words and pictures. Teachers may record these responses on sentence strips.

ANALYZING THE PARTS OF A WHOLE

Directions for Elementary Students

Step One: Name the object.

Step Two: Name the different parts of the object.

Step Three: Choose a part of the object and talk about what the part does and what would happen if that part were not there. Repeat for all the important parts.

Step Four: Say a few sentences about the object and its parts.

ANALYZING THE PARTS OF A WHOLE

Directions for Secondary Students

Step One: Identify the whole.

Step Two: Identify the parts of the whole.

Step Three: For each part, identify its function and what would happen if that part were not there.

Step Four: Use all the information to state an interpretation or summary to describe how the parts contribute to the whole.

INCORPORATING ANALYZING THE PARTS OF A WHOLE INTO LESSONS

You can use this skill to teach concepts or systems in any curriculum content. Physical objects, biological systems, mathematical equations, theories, sentences in either English or in a foreign language, charts, political cartoons, graphs, and tables can be broken down and examined in terms of their component parts.

Once students know the skill, you can use it in a number of ways. You may assign different groups to take different parts and share their findings with the larger group. Alternatively, you may ask students to work with particular parts from the list produced. These may be the parts that students need to demonstrate an understanding of in order to meet a state standard or answer questions on a standardized test. For example:

- Demonstrate an understanding of plot, point of view, setting, conflict, and character for English Language Arts.

- Label and identify the function of the petal, stigma, style, and stamen for life science.

- Understand the function of various terms in different formulas and equations, graphs, and geometrical shapes for mathematics.

Once students have mastery of Analyzing the Parts of a Whole, they can use it in any situation they face with something they do not understand. They can break down the problem at hand and look at the component parts to try to understand it.

SAMPLE ANALYZING THE PARTS OF A WHOLE ACTIVITIES

MATHEMATICS

- a simple number sentence
- parts of a polygon or three dimensional shape
- a graph, chart, matrix, or table
- a mathematical diagram
- a mathematical equation (simple or complex)
- different mathematical formulae
- an angle
- word problems
- fractions

ENGLISH LANGUAGE ARTS

- plot, character, setting, etc. as applied to a particular story
- parts of speech
- parts of a dictionary
- a simple sentence
- a picture book, novel, or textbook
- parts of a report or essay
- parts of a story as applied to a particular novel
- characters in a story
- sections of a formal or informal letter
- lines of an address

SOCIAL STUDIES

- parts of a globe or map
- different components of a society or aspects of culture
- geographical make up of a country (e.g., desert, mountains, coast)
- The Constitution of the United States
- governments
- colonial or medieval villages
- cities, neighborhoods
- economic systems
- political systems
- judicial systems

SCIENCE

- a plant or seed
- an electric circuit
- an atom
- different body organs or systems
- an electromagnet
- The Solar System
- an ecosystem

- layers of Earth's surface
- periodic table
- tools (e.g., microscopes, telescopes)

LEARNING A LANGUAGE
(English Language Learners or Learning a Foreign Language)

- different verb forms and tenses
- the structure of a sentence in a different language
- break down simple objects to learn vocabulary

PHYSICAL EDUCATION

- a sneaker
- a game
- a healthy lifestyle
- skills required to play a sport competently
- a team

THE ARTS

- a musical instrument (e.g., violin, piano, clarinet)
- a painting
- an orchestra
- sections in a play, piece of music, or dance
- elements of design

TECHNOLOGY

- a computer
- word processing screen
- Internet page
- different functions of an electronic device
- parts of an e-mail or Internet address

FREQUENTLY ASKED QUESTIONS ABOUT
ANALYZING THE PARTS OF A WHOLE

My students use a reference to identify the parts of the item. Then they use the reference to identify the function of each part. They are simply filling in the blanks. However, then they want me to tell them what to put in the other sections of the graphic organizer. How do I get them to use this skill to develop meaning and understanding rather than to fill in blanks?

Tell students to complete only the first two steps of the skill using the reference. Have them put the reference away, and verbalize for themselves what would happen if the part were not there, and restate the function of the part. Encourage them to state the responses independently.

What do I do when students cannot describe what happens if the part is not there?

Have a range of resources available for students to complete this step of the skill.

Birds of a Feather: Teaching the Structured Thinking Skill of Categorizing and Grouping in the Student-Centered Classroom

The aim of the educator should be to teach how to think, rather than what to think.

—John Dewey

BIRDS OF A FEATHER: TEACHING THE STRUCTURED THINKING SKILL OF CATEGORIZING AND GROUPING IN THE STUDENT-CENTERED CLASSROOM

10

Categorizing and Grouping are two of the most basic mental processes. We continually make sense of the world around us by organizing information and things. We use the term *Grouping* when we create categories into which to place items. For example, to organize a collection items collected in the woods, a child might use Grouping to create the following categories: animal parts, rocks, and plant parts. *Categorizing* is what we do when we actually place items into the categories that we have created or that are already established. Our child in the above example might now use Categorizing to place each of her treasures into one of her three categories.

When we go to the supermarket and want to buy milk, we know to look in the dairy aisle. If we want to buy a book, we go to a bookstore or the book department of another store. We have places in our homes where we put particular things. For example, we usually find a stove in the kitchen, knives in the cutlery drawer, and so on. Imagine the chaos that there would be if we did not organize things in a sensible way.

CATEGORIZING AND GROUPING ENABLES STUDENTS TO:

- analyze information from all sources in a meaningful way.

- set up organized systems for the storage and retrieval of information.

- organize information into categories that are useful for test preparation and for formulating a well-structured piece of writing.

- develop an understanding of standard classification systems.

- seek clarification when they do not understand something.

- develop clarity in the use of language.

TEACHING THE STRUCTURED THINKING SKILL OF CATEGORIZING

Introducing the Skill

When introducing this skill tell students that they are going to learn a skill that they experience daily—whether they are at the library, at the music store, in the classroom, or at the supermarket. Ask them to think about the music store and the different categories of compact disks (CDs) there. Hold up a variety of CDs or items from the supermarket and ask students where they would find them in the store. Explain to students that stores use categorization to place similar items together. The goal of categorization is to find the best fit.

Explain that when we use this type of thinking, we may be doing one of two things: categorizing or classifying. The skill that they are going to start with is Categorizing.

First Step in Skill
Identify what you are sorting.
Record what students are going to sort: a set of quadrilaterals, different modes of transport, a set of letter blends, or words and phrases that mean the same as "good."

Second Step in Skill
Identify the categories into which the objects can be placed and the characteristics for each category.
Ask students to examine each category and describe the characteristics.

Sample Responses for *Sorting Quadrilaterals:*

The categories are rectangles, trapezoids, and parallelograms.	
Category	**Key characteristics**
Rectangles	Four straight sides, two pairs of parallel sides, four right angles
Trapezoids	Four straight sides, one pair of parallel sides
Parallelograms	Two pairs of parallel sides, no right angles

Third Step in Skill
Consider each item and describe its characteristics. Place each item and explain why you chose that category.
The second part of the step is to ask students to place items in the appropriate category verbalizing why as they do so.

 POINTER: Ensure that students verbalize at each step of the skill.

Sample Responses for *Sorting Quadrilaterals*:

Shape	Verbal description
	This shape has four right angles and two pairs of parallel sides of different lengths so it goes in the category of **rectangle**. It is an oblong.
	This shape has two obtuse and two acute angles. It has one pair of parallel sides and goes in the category of **trapezoid**.
	This shape has two pairs of parallel sides that are of equal length. It has no right angles. It goes into the category of **parallelogram**.
	This shape has four equal sides and four right angles. It has two pairs of parallel sides. It goes into the category of **rectangle**. It is a square.

 POINTER: Ensure that students are talking to each other and not reporting to the teacher.

Fourth Step in Skill

Use all the information to state an interpretation or summary about the items and categories and what you have learned by categorizing in this way.

Ask students to share their summary statements and thank them without making a value statement. Once the sharing has taken place, give individuals time to make any amendments and make sure that their notes are clear. Students can work individually or in TAPPS pairs.

 POINTER: **Explain that all summary statements are valid.**

When the skill or this way of working is new to students, they may find forming summary statements and interpretations difficult. Explain to them that they cannot get this wrong; their summary statement is their interpretation of the content. As they become more experienced with writing them and listening to other students, summary statements do become more sophisticated.

Sample Summary Statement for Categorizing *Quadrilaterals*:

Quadrilaterals are four-sided polygons that you can place into different groups depending on the type of angle and type and length of sides.

In the preceding example, students have organized the information and made their own meaning. They can explain why they did what they did. The verbalization of the thinking is crucial; it will ensure that students really think about where they are placing items.

CATEGORIZING

Directions for Elementary Students

Step One: What are you sorting?

Step Two: What are the categories that you are using to sort the items? What are the characteristics of the category?

Step Three: Place each of the items into the best category and explain why you have chosen that category.

Step Four: In a few sentences, say something about what you did.

CATEGORIZING

Directions for Secondary Students

Step One: Identify what you are sorting.

Step Two: Identify the categories into which the objects can be placed and the characteristics for each category.

Step Three: Consider each item and describe its characteristics. Place each item and explain why you chose that category.

Step Four: Use all the information to state an interpretation or summary about the items and categories and what you have learned by categorizing in this way.

TEACHING THE STRUCTURED THINKING SKILL OF GROUPING

Introducing the Skill

Tell students that today they are going to learn the Structured Thinking Skill of Grouping. They have already learned that Categorizing is the Structured Thinking Skill to use to place objects in categories that already exist. Ask students to list any situations in which this happens. Remind them of the music store or supermarket.

Explain that when we use the Structured Thinking Skill of Grouping to create a classification system, the person doing the sorting creates the categories. Ask students to think about something they have organized: their bedroom at home, a CD collection, or the files on a computer. Ask them how they did it. How did they decide what went where? Ask students to share.

When teaching this skill, give students the items or information to group. These may be physical objects such as buttons, plants, or shapes. These may also be something more abstract such a set of numbers, information contained in a body of text (for example, products produced in a particular country, a list of vocabulary associated with the topic of photosynthesis, or a collection of foodstuffs that come from plants). Students can use this skill to organize any body of information.

Example using foodstuffs that come from plants:

Have a selection of edible plants, e.g., carrot, turnip, lettuce, tomato, rhubarb, almond, and cucumber.

First Step in Skill
Consider each object and describe its characteristics.

Sample responses:

Carrot	Tomato	Cucumber
Key characteristics: Orange Root of the plant Can be eaten raw or cooked	*Key characteristics:* Red Fruit of plant Can be eaten raw or cooked	*Key characteristics:* Fruit Green Usually eaten raw

Rhubarb	Lettuce	Almond
Key characteristics: Leaves are poisonous Stem of the plant Red/ Green color Eaten cooked, usually sweetened	*Key characteristics:* Green Leaf of plant Usually eaten raw	*Key characteristics:* Seed of the plant Eaten either raw or cooked Brown

Second Step in Skill

Identify possible groupings that you could use and explain the significance of grouping this way.

The second part of the step is to ask students to identify some ways they could group the items and explain the significance of grouping in this way.

Sample responses:

> "If I grouped them according to color, I would see that there are only certain colors. My categories are orange, green, red, and brown."

> "I could group them according to the part of the plant that we eat to understand which parts of a plant we eat. My categories are leaf, stem, root, fruit, and seed."

> "I could group them according to how they are prepared as a foodstuff to learn more about their culinary use. My categories are generally eaten raw, generally eaten cooked, and eaten both raw and cooked."

> "I could group them according to their caloric count to examine those that would be suitable for consumption on a weight reducing diet. My categories are 0-50 calories per oz., 50-100 calories per 4oz., 100-150 per 4 oz. 150-200 calories per oz., 200-250 calories per oz., and 250-300 calories per oz."

Third Step in Skill

State an interpretation or summary about the grouping you are going to use.

Ask students to select a classification system to use to group the plants and explain why they have made that choice. Ask them to identify the categories into which they will place the item.

Sample response:

> "I am going to group these plants according to the parts that we eat to highlight the fact that we eat different parts of different plants. The categories are leaf, stem, root, fruit, and seed."

Students can stop at this point or go on to Categorize to find the best fit for each of the vegetables. Different groups could work with different ways of categorizing the plant foodstuffs.

Sample response:

What I am grouping:		
Plant Food Stuffs according to the part of the plant that we eat		
Category	**Characteristics**	**Members of the category**
Leaf	Generally green Foliage part of plant	Lettuce
Stem	Long, thin Supports the leaves	Rhubarb
Root	Grows underground Generally tapered	Carrot
Fruit	Surrounds the seed Formed from the flower	Cucumber, tomato
Seed	Starts in the fruit Often nut-like	Almond

Once students have the foodstuffs you could extend the activity and ask them to find more members for each of the categories.

Sample response:

Things to be grouped:		
Plant Food Stuffs according to the part of the plant that we eat		
Category	**Key characteristics**	**Additional members of the category**
Leaf	Generally green Foliage part of plant	Lettuce, arugula, endive, cabbage
Stem	Long, thin Has leaves growing off it	Rhubarb, celery, scallions, asparagus
Root	Grows underground Generally tapered	Carrot, turnip, parsnip, radish
Fruit	Surrounds the seed Formed from the flower	Cucumber, tomato, apple, orange, peach
Seed	Starts in the fruit of the plant Often nut or pulses	Almond, peas, walnut, broad bean

Fourth Step In Skill
Group the items using Categorizing.
The next step is to ask students to write a summary statement or interpretation.

Sample response:

> Plants provide us with a wide range of food. Grouping in this way made me think about the different parts of the plant that we eat. I found that for most plants we only eat one particular part.

 POINTER: Stay neutral to develop students' independence.

> Remember not to make any value judgments, such as saying "good" to specific students, as this will have a negative effect on those to whom you do not say it. Just thank participants for their summary statements.

Students can share their summary statements in smaller groups. It is important that everyone attempt to write something. Remind students that writing summary statements will become easier over time and that the more we do something, the better we get.

GROUPING

Directions for Elementary Students

Step One: Look at each item and describe it.

Step Two: Say some ways you could group them. What would your categories be?

Step Three: In a few sentences, say something about what you did.

Step Four: Now Categorize the items.

GROUPING

Directions for Secondary Students

Step One: Consider each object and describe its characteristics.

Step Two: Identify possible groupings that you could use and explain the significance of grouping this way.

Step Three: State an interpretation or summary about the grouping you are going to use.

Step Four: Group the items using the Structured Thinking Skill of Categorizing.

INCORPORATING GROUPING INTO LESSONS

You can use this skill with content from all curriculum areas as the main learning activity of a lesson, as a short introductory activity, or as a closing activity.

 POINTERS

> **Use Grouping to activate and assess prior knowledge.**
> When embarking on a new topic (e.g., photosynthesis, trigonometry, people in the community that help us, etc.), have students verbalize a definition of the topic and categories or groupings within it. This will help students connect with the new topic, give you an indication of their level of understanding, and provide a foundation for future learning.

> **Use Grouping for review.**
> The skill is an excellent technique for students to review what they have learned at the end of a lesson or topic (e.g., list all vocabulary related to the human heart, the art of Pablo Picasso, the music of George Gershwin, etc. and create categories or groupings to organize it in a meaningful way). Students can use the skill to review for standardized tests.

SAMPLE CATEGORIZING AND GROUPING ACTIVITIES

MATHEMATICS

- two-dimensional and three-dimensional figures
- right, obtuse, and acute angles
- characteristics of different quadrilaterals
- odd and even numbers
- numbers (e.g., decimals, fractional, prime, square, and triangular)
- numbers by multiples
- different equations
- types of graphs or charts
- sets of coins

ENGLISH LANGUAGE ARTS

- genres of literature; authors
- types of fiction
- types of writing: expository, descriptive, narrative, persuasive
- collections of books
- types of poetry
- story characters (e.g., fairy tale heroes and villains)
- parts of speech
- words by language of origin (e.g., Latin, Anglo-Saxon, or Bantu)
- kinds of figurative language
- ads and advertising techniques
- books and the Dewey Decimal System

SOCIAL STUDIES

- rooms in the home; items found in the home
- vocabulary and symbols associated with geographical and topographical maps
- geographical features (e.g., land forms and bodies of water)

- terms associated with water features: rivers, streams, meanders, levees, oxbow, lake, and flood)
- jobs in the community
- different forms of economic activity
- countries according to continent, languages spoken, climate, or land use
- domestic items, housing, transport into the era that they were produced
- leaders by political philosophy

SCIENCE

- types of rock
- weather elements and cloud types
- living and nonliving materials
- states of matter (e.g., liquid, solid, gas)
- terms associated with light (e.g., refracted, reflected, absorbed, visible light, ultraviolet radiation)
- animal species by genera, family, order, or phylum
- foods according to different food groups
- chemical elements
- conductors of electricity
- different types of energy (e.g., light, heat, sound, chemical, nuclear, and electrical)
- items in an ecosystem

LEARNING A LANGUAGE
(English Language Learners or Learning a Foreign Language)

- vocabulary (e.g., words associated with shopping, school, going on vacation, movement, emotions, family, numbers, foodstuffs, sports, computers, playing, swimming, and going to the beach)
- verbs according to tense or form
- aspects of life in a country where the language is spoken
- objects by their different colors, shapes, or sizes, etc.

- collections of everyday objects (e.g., clothing, tableware, and stationery items)
- greetings
- completing the steps in the skill in the different language

PHYSICAL EDUCATION

- sports
- types of physical exercise
- gymnastic movements
- components of a health-related fitness plan
- team, paired, and individual sports
- classify chemical substances according to their use
- types of contraception
- types of disease
- equipment needed for different sports (e.g., tennis, volleyball, horseback riding, swimming, football, or soccer)

THE ARTS

- types and styles of music (e.g., classical, pop, jazz)
- musical terms
- musical notes (e.g., whole notes, half notes, quarter notes, dotted notes, etc.)
- types of world music
- orchestral instruments (e.g., woodwind, string, percussion, brass)
- art styles and media (e.g., sculpture, painting, etching drawing, printing, photography)
- artistic movements
- types of dance (e.g., tap, ballet, swing, tango)
- works of art by the same artist

TECHNOLOGY

- ways of communicating

- media sources

- organize computer files into appropriate categories

- systems for storing Internet favorites

- applications (e.g., graphic, word processing, database, spreadsheet)

- types of Internet sites (e.g., museums, search engines)

- sources of information (e.g., Internet site, CD Rom, computer disk, books, video)

- uses of a computer

FREQUENTLY ASKED QUESTIONS ABOUT CATEGORIZING AND GROUPING

My students do not understand when to use Categorizing and when to use Grouping. How can I clarify this for my students?

Explain to students that there is a difference between *understanding* a classification or grouping system already in place and *creating* their own. If students are using a classification or grouping system that is already in place and sorting items into its categories, they are using the Structured Thinking Skill of Categorizing. Students must understand the classification systems that we use (for example, the Dewey Decimal System, the Periodic Table of Elements, the Linnaean System of Nomenclature, etc.) and use them to build on their knowledge. If students are creating a classification or grouping system (gathering individual items into larger groups of items) they are using the Structured Thinking Skill of Grouping. Students create groupings when they want to organize their ideas.

What is the difference between mind mapping and grouping?

We usually use mind mapping to organize and communicate information and ideas in a subjective, personal way without using specific rules. In Grouping, students use discrete steps, for example, identifying the categories and the characteristics of each category.

Getting Your Ducks in a Row: Teaching the Structured Thinking Skill of Ordering in the Student-Centered Classroom

*Everything should be made as simple
as possible, but not simpler.*

—Albert Einstein

GETTING YOUR DUCKS IN A ROW: TEACHING THE STRUCTURED THINKING SKILL OF ORDERING IN THE STUDENT-CENTERED CLASSROOM

11

We are so accustomed to Ordering, we are not even aware that we are doing it. We seldom realize that we are ordering in different ways while performing everyday activities.

We use the skill of ordering or sequencing constantly in our everyday lives. We order in three main ways:

- **by Time:** we place things in order by time (e.g., by year, month, day, hour, etc.)

- **by Occurrence:** we place related steps in order, showing how one leads to another (e.g., steps in a recipe or instructions for a game)

- **by Rank:** we create an order using a specific criterion against which we can measure and rank things (e.g., from shortest to longest, most to least important, numeric or alphabetical order, etc.)

Think of the process of making a Thanksgiving turkey dinner: tasks you must complete and the order in which you must do them for everything to be ready at the same time. During your preparations, you will Order by *Time*, *Occurrence*, and *Rank*.

You must order by *Time* many of your chores so that you allow enough time to get everything done. The day before you buy the turkey, flowers for the table, and get the final head count for dinner. Early on Thanksgiving morning you make the stuffing, stuff the turkey, and put the turkey in the oven. Late Thanksgiving morning you set the table, arrange the flowers, and prepare the vegetables. In early afternoon, you prepare the salad. An hour before you serve dinner, you cook the vegetables. Just before you serve the meal at four o'clock, you make the gravy and dress the salad. You place the hot food on the table, sit, and your family enjoys a delicious meal. You managed your time well.

You could organize the same jobs by the order in which they *occur* without specific times. You might do this as a planning exercise or if different people are going to take on different tasks. For example, you could arrange the flowers on Thanksgiving morning or on the day before. You may decide to shop two days before. This type of ordering addresses the order and relationship between different things. For example, you could think about the turkey: You must buy it, prepare the stuffing, stuff the turkey, cook the turkey, make the gravy, serve the turkey, and eat.

You could think about the vegetables: You must wash and prepare them. You must cook the hot vegetables, serve them, and eat them. You must wash, combine, dress, and serve the salad ingredients and then eat the salad.

The other items have to do with hospitality. You need to check who is coming for dinner so that you know how many places to set at the table. You need to buy the flowers, arrange them, and place them on the dining table, and so on.

You may also decide to order the jobs by *Rank* from the most to the least important. This ranking helps you to prioritize if, for example, you begin to run out of time.

- The *most important tasks* are buying and cooking the turkey, as the turkey is the fundamental ingredient of a Thanksgiving dinner. Setting the table will come next as people need a place to eat. Buying and cooking the hot vegetables is also important so people will have a healthy, balanced meal.
- Of *medium importance* is the preparation and serving of the salad. People will have plenty of vegetables; the weather is cold so hot vegetables will be more fortifying.
- *Least important* is the buying and arranging flowers. These would make the table look more attractive but they are not an essential part of the meal.

THE STRUCTURED THINKING SKILL OF ORDERING ENABLES STUDENTS TO:

- understand the different types of Ordering (by Time, Rank, and Occurrence) and how they are used.

- explain the different criteria that they may use when placing things in order.

- organize the information processed during other Structured Thinking Skills to formulate well-structured pieces of writing.

- plan for both the long and short term by identifying related actions and the tasks needed to complete them.

- explain the reasons for liking something or thinking something is an important or a major influence.

- make decisions about the degree of importance or degree of influence.

- write a well-sequenced narrative.

- manage time and prioritize.

TEACHING THE STRUCTURED THINKING SKILL OF ORDERING BY TIME

When first teaching the skill, tell students that they are going to learn the Structured Thinking Skill of Ordering by Time.

Introducing the Skill

Ordering by Time refers to placing events in the order they occurred or when they are planned or predicted to occur. We use chronological order to make sense of what has happened and what we need to do. Draw a timeline on the board starting in the year that the oldest student was born. At the end of the timeline, write the current year. Ask students to think about their own lives and sequence some of the important events that have happened. For example, they can list when they were born, when brothers and sisters were born, when they learned to ride a bike, when they started school, and so on. Have them create their own timeline. Explain that they can examine many events this way.

Ordering by Time utilizes commonly understood intervals, e.g., by the hour, day, decade, century, or millennium. Students may be able to think of other examples.

First Step in Skill

Identify what you are ordering and why.

As an introductory activity, ask students to list as many of the different celebrations and holidays that they can think of. Working in pairs, they may come up with a list like the following: Labor Day, Cinco de Mayo, Christmas Day, Hanukkah, Eid al Fitr, Memorial Day, Independence Day, Thanksgiving Day, and New Year's Day.

Tell students that they are going to use the skill of Ordering by Time to organize the celebrations and holidays according to when they occur throughout the year. Beginning with the first step of the skill, students will state what they are sequencing, state the type of sequencing they are using, and then place the items in order.

Example using *Festivals and Holidays*:

> I am ordering different holidays and celebrations by arranging them according to the calendar to examine the time of year that they occur.

 POINTER: Make it tangible.

> Students can write down what they are ordering on individual cards or Post-its® so that they can move them around easily.

Second Step in Skill

Identify the type of ordering that fits this purpose.

Ask students to identify the type of ordering that they are using. In this case, they are ordering by time using the months of the year.

Example using *Festivals and Holidays:*

> I am ordering the different festivals and holidays by time according to the when during the year they occur.

Timelines can take many different forms. You can draw them horizontally or vertically and in the form of a line or table.

Third Step In Skill
Place the events or actions in order according to the interval of time in which they happened or you expect them to happen.
Ask students to place the events in order according to when they occur during the year.

Sample response using *Festivals and Holidays*:

My sequence is as follows:

Date/Time	Event/Activity
January	New Year's Day
February	
March	
April	
May	Cinco de Mayo, Memorial Day
June	
July	Independence Day
August	
September	Labor Day
October	
November	Diwali, Thanksgiving Day
December	Hanukkah, Eid al Fitr, Christmas Day

When students have completed their timelines, ask them to share their responses in pairs, small groups, or with the large group. Another way that students can share timelines is to post them on the wall for a "gallery walk" in which students walk around, read, and perhaps comment on what their fellow students did. Students will produce a variety of different timelines. Students can discuss what they have learned from each other in an Effective Group Process discussion following sharing.

 POINTER: Ensure that students are talking to each other, not reporting to the teacher.

When students are sharing their ideas with each other, they are not reporting what they did to you, the teacher.

Fourth Step In Skill

Use all the information to state an interpretation or summary regarding the significance of the order.

The final stage of the process is to have students write a summary statement or interpretation.

 POINTER: **Remember to accept all conclusions.**

Sample Summary Statement using *Festivals and Holidays*:

Christmas, New Years Day, Cinco de Mayo, and Independence Day are the only holidays that fall on the same date every year. Memorial Day, Labor Day, Hanukkah, and Diwali tend to be in the same month every year. The Moslem calendar is based on the lunar cycle, which means that the Festival of Eid al Fitr occurs earlier on the Roman calendar during each subsequent year. The exact date is not known in advance as it depends on the sighting of a new moon.

ORDERING BY TIME

<u>Directions for Elementary Students</u>

Step One: Describe what you are ordering.

Step Two: Place the events in order and explain what you are doing.

Step Three: In a few sentences, say something about when the events happened.

ORDERING BY TIME

<u>Directions for Secondary Students</u>

Step One: Identify what you are ordering and why.

Step Two: Identify the type of ordering that fits this purpose.

Step Three: Place the events or actions in order according to the interval of time in which they happened or you expect them to happen.

Step Four: Use all the information to state an interpretation or summary regarding the significance of the order.

TEACHING THE STRUCTURED THINKING SKILL OF ORDERING BY OCCURRENCE

Introducing the Skill

When introducing this skill to students, say that this is another type of ordering. When we Order by Time we are using standard, commonly understood intervals such as years, months, or days. Sometimes we must carry out actions or events in a particular order but not necessarily at a particular time. For example, ask students to talk through the steps to set a VCR to tape a TV program, make a peanut butter and jelly sandwich, or walk to school. You must follow the steps in a particular order. If not, it is likely that you will not get to watch the TV program, the sandwich will be a sticky disaster, and you will not make it to school.

Have someone share the order he or she created and write the steps on the chalkboard. Alternatively, ask students to pair up and follow their partner's steps to see if the instructions are clear and easy to follow.

When teaching Ordering by Occurrence, the life cycle of a butterfly is a good introductory activity. Take students through the steps. Tell students they are going to use the skill of Ordering by Occurrence and produce a chart for their notebooks. Students can also create the chart using a computer drawing application.

First Step in Skill

Identify what you are ordering and why.

Provide students with a text or series of pictures to Order by Occurrence, for example, egg, butterfly, cocoon, and caterpillar. Ask them to examine the text or pictures and identify what it is that they are ordering and why.

Sample response:

> I am ordering the stages of development in the life cycle of a butterfly to examine the different stages that it goes through.

Second Step in Skill

Identify the type of ordering that fits this purpose.

Explain that we use Ordering by Occurrence to examine life cycles, procedures, and processes where we do **not** consider specific time intervals. In this example, students are examining a life cycle.

Sample response:

> Ordering by Occurrence fits this purpose.

Third Step in Skill

Place the events or actions in order and explain the relationship between the steps. Describe what would happen if you omitted a particular step or included one that was incomplete.

Now ask students to place the events in order.

Sample response:

Egg Stage
The butterfly starts life as an egg that hatches and out comes a caterpillar.

Caterpillar Stage
The caterpillar eats lots of green leaves and gets very fat. When it is fully grown it forms a pupa or chrysalis.

Pupa or Chrysalis Stage
From the outside, everything looks very quiet but inside there is big changes are happening. This is called metamorphosis. The case is called a cocoon.

Butterfly
From the cocoon, there emerges a beautiful butterfly. The butterfly flies around, mates with another butterfly and the female butterfly lays eggs.

Ask students to examine their orderings, consider each step, and verbalize what would happen if they omitted or disturbed a step. This will help them focus on the relationship of a particular step to the whole process.
Sample responses:

If the egg stage were missing or incomplete, there would be no beginning to the process. A butterfly reproduces by laying eggs that hatch into caterpillars.

If the caterpillar stage were missing, there would be no larval stage in the cycle. The caterpillar eats a lot and builds up energy for the next stage in the process.

If the pupa stage were missing or incomplete, there would be no period where the metamorphosis occurs. This is when the caterpillar becomes a butterfly.

If the butterfly stage were missing or incomplete, there would be no adult stage in the life cycle. The adult would not be able to mate and lay the eggs that become the new generation.

Fourth Step In Skill
Use all the information to state an interpretation or summary regarding the significance of the order.

The final step in the skill is to write a summary statement or interpretation.

Sample Summary Statement for *Ordering by Occurrence the Life Cycle of a Butterfly:*

The life cycle of the butterfly goes around in a circle beginning and ending with an egg.

Students can then use this information to make a poster or chart. They could then find out about the life cycle of different organisms, for example, a frog, chick, cow, or kangaroo. The mental steps that they go through would be the same, though the content would be different.

147

ORDERING BY OCCURRENCE

Directions for Elementary Students

Step One: Tell what you are ordering.

Step Two: Place the events or actions in order. Talk about the relationship between the steps. What would happen if you skipped a step?

Step Three: In a few sentences, say something about the order of the events.

ORDERING BY OCCURRENCE

Directions for Secondary Students

Step One: Identify what you are ordering and why.

Step Two: Identify the type of ordering that fits this purpose.

Step Three: Place the events or actions in order and explain the relationship between the steps. Describe what would happen if you omitted a particular step or included one that was incomplete.

Step Four: Use all the information to state an interpretation or summary regarding the significance of the order.

TEACHING THE STRUCTURED THINKING SKILL OF ORDERING BY RANK

Introducing the Skill

Tell students that this is another of the three types of ordering for organizing information that will be very familiar to them.

To demonstrate this skill, use a set of nesting boxes, Russian dolls, or different-sized oranges. Ask a student to put them in order and explain the criteria that he or she selected. The student will probably place them in order of size, from smallest to largest. Say that this type of ordering, Ordering by Rank, is one in which things are arranged according to a specified criterion.

In record stores, we may see a display of the Top Ten videos or DVDs. These are usually the ten best-selling items in the category. This is a form of Ordering by Rank.

POINTER: **Introduce Ordering by Rank using objective criteria.**

To introduce the skill, start simple and ask students to think about ranking something using objective criteria. For example, rank the most popular children's movies in the country that week according to the figures published in a daily newspaper.

First Step in Skill
Identify what is being ordered and why.

Sample response using *Current Children's Movies*:

I am going to use Ordering by Rank to determine the most popular children's movies.

Second Step in Skill
Identify the type of ordering that fits this purpose.

Sample response using *Current Children's Movies*:

I am using Ordering by Rank to order this information.

Third Step in Skill
Identify the criteria for the ranking.

Sample response using *Current Children's Movies:*

The criterion for this ranking is the number of tickets sold or the amount of money earned at the box office.

Fourth Step in Skill
Place the items in order according to how they meet the criteria. State the reasons.

Sample response using *Current Children's Movies:*

The most popular movie is_____ with _____ tickets sold.
The second most popular movie is _____ with _____ tickets sold.

Fifth Step in Skill
Use all the information to state an interpretation or summary regarding the significance of the order.

Sample response using *Current Children's Movies:*

The three most popular children's movies are either animated movies or comedies.

Introducing a More Complex Ordering by Rank Using Subjective Criteria

When we ranked popular children's movies, listing the important criteria was relatively easy. We had information about the number of tickets sold. When students are first using the skill, they may find it harder to verbalize the important criteria when thinking about factors that are more subjective. Ask students to list their three most favorite movies. They need to list the criteria that they are going to use to complete the ranking.

Their criteria may include things like the following:

- If it makes me laugh or cry

- If it focuses on everyday life

- If it is set in New York City

- If the cast is good looking

- If it has a good soundtrack

- If it has good special effects

- If it stars one of my favorite actors

Students really have to think about the films and determine to what degree they meet their criteria. Their top movie may meet all the criteria. Their second may meet all but one of the criteria; the third may meet three of the criteria. They have gone through a thought process that will allow them to communicate this. We often state what we like but have not systematically thought out the reasons why.

 POINTER: Accept all criteria.

Remember that the criteria that students select may not be the ones that you would choose. This does not matter. It is going through the thought process that is the important thing.

Students then select their most popular films, verbalizing why they have chosen each one. They can then write a summary statement.

Try doing this yourself for your favorite books or way to relax and you will see that it is a complex task.

Once students have mastered the skill, they will understand that sometimes the criteria are more objective (e.g., heaviest to lightest, position along a line of latitude from north to south, using numeric or alphabetical order) and sometimes they are more subjective (e.g., determining the major influences of a writer, or the greatest labor saving device).

ORDERING BY RANK

Directions for Elementary Students

Step One: You are going to put these things in order from the_____
to the _____.

Step Two: Place the things in order and give the reasons you ordered
them as you did.

Step Three: In a few sentences, say something about the order and the
ranking.

- OR -

Step One: Describe what you are you placing in order. Say what type
of order you are using.

Step Two: Place the things in order and give the reasons why you
ordered them this way.

Step Three: In a few sentences, say something about the order and the
ranking.

ORDERING BY RANK

Directions for Secondary Students

Step One: Identify what you are ordering and why.

Step Two: Identify the type of ordering that fits this purpose.

Step Three: Identify the criteria for ranking

Step Four: Place the items in order according to how they meet the
criteria. State the reasons.

Step Five: Use all the information to state an interpretation or
summary regarding the significance of the order.

INCORPORATING ORDERING INTO LESSONS

The skill of Ordering can be used in many areas of the curriculum.

 POINTER: **Be clear about which type of ordering you are using.**

When working with this skill, clearly define the type of sequencing you are using. If you do not make it clear, students may become confused. For example, you can sequence the events that led up to the American Civil War by Time or you can sequence them by rank from the most to least significant. The mental steps are different depending on the type of ordering you use.

You can use Ordering by Time to examine a person's life, the development of a country, different geological periods, the development of different inventions, or the development of different theories. Students can use this skill to reflect on their development as learners:

- to create timelines of themselves as readers or learners of English.

- to review the sequence they used to learn different topics.

- as a time-management tool.

Students can use Ordering by Occurrence to examine different scientific or mathematical processes or to organize the order of paragraphs in an essay. You can use it to check students' comprehension of works of fiction.

You can incorporate Ordering by Rank into every curriculum area (e.g., sorting numbers from the highest to lowest in mathematics, analyzing the main causes of the Great Depression, determining the most popular children's books, ranking foods according to their caloric content, etc.). Students can use this skill as a self-management tool for prioritizing what they must accomplish.

SAMPLE ORDERING BY TIME ACTIVITIES

Ordering by Time

MATHEMATICS

- events in a typical day

- planning a schedule so that a list of jobs can be done

- collecting and reporting data over time (e.g., traffic surveys, daily temperature, attendance)

- scheduling personal time

ENGLISH LANGUAGE ARTS

- events in a story, film, or comic strip
- aligning or correlating an author's works to important dates
- relating different literary movements to social, philosophical, or artistic trends
- relating biographical details of an individual's life to significant external events
- changes in a character during the course of a story

SOCIAL STUDIES

- relating generations on a family tree to various decades
- organizing significant historic events (e.g., main events in the Cultural Revolution in China or the American Civil War) to clarify the pace and duration of change or their relation to other historical events or conditions
- events in a historical figure's life
- changes in maps and boundaries to highlight the establishment of different countries
- activities in the daily life of a Sioux Indian child

SCIENCE

- development of different scientific theories
- dating different scientific discoveries
- stages of development of individual plant, animal, or human life cycle
- history of space travel
- evolution of the universe
- relating seasons and weather to the calendar

LEARNING A LANGUAGE
(English Language Learners or Learning a Foreign Language)

- learning vocabulary for time, i.e. days, months, and seasons
- relating the history of the country where the language is spoken to other historical events
- creating a calendar of birthdays or other special events in the different language

- recording events of the previous or upcoming day, weekend, or week
- creating a homework schedule

PHYSICAL EDUCATION

- documenting events in a game or match
- creating an exercise routine
- dating major sporting events or athletic achievements

THE ARTS

- comparing works of an artist, composer, playwright, or filmmaker to concurrent world events
- development of an artistic movement, period, or era

TECHNOLOGY

- relating technological developments to each other and to historical, social, and cultural events
- recording and evaluating time spent on different computer activities

Ordering by Occurrence

MATHEMATICS

- steps in different mathematical operations (e.g., addition, subtraction, division, or multiplication)
- explaining the steps when solving a mathematical problem
- algebraic order of operations
- clarifying the steps in working out the mean, median, and mode in order to interpret data, assure accuracy, and prevent confusion

ENGLISH LANGUAGE ARTS

- retelling the main events in the plot of a story
- determining the steps in writing reports

- determining and differentiating the prewriting steps for narratives or research reports
- rules and procedures for playing a board game
- clarifying the steps in ordinary activities (e.g., making a cup of tea, drawing a graph, or making a sandwich)

SOCIAL STUDIES

- describing one's route to school
- steps in the electoral process
- depicting the generations in a family
- tracking the development of an invention
- changing roles played by women in society

SCIENCE

- describing chemical reactions
- explaining the life cycle of a butterfly to understand metamorphosis
- building an electrical circuit
- explaining water, carbon, nitrogen, and phosphorus cycles
- bodily processes (e.g., reproductive cycle, digestion, or excretion)

FOREIGN LANGUAGE

- writing simple instructions
- completing the steps in the skill in the different language
- explaining how to buy a particular item
- following instructions in a different language (e.g., for a word processing application)

PHYSICAL EDUCATION

- clarifying the correct body position in a forward roll
- executing a particular type of throw or movement
- training procedures in a particular sport or game

- describing the menstrual cycle
- dance

THE ARTS

- making of art or craft work
- explaining the stages an artist or composer went through to produce a piece of art or music
- learning to play a musical instrument
- explaining the plot of an opera, ballet, or play

TECHNOLOGY

- opening, writing, saving a document
- turning on or shutting down a computer
- writing and sending an e-mail
- using a digital camera
- explaining the steps in a particular computer application

Ordering by Rank

MATHEMATICS

- order the units used in measuring (e.g., weight, length, time, volume, or temperature)
- order shapes according to size (e.g., number of sides, number of angles, area, or perimeter)
- depicting the value of different fractions
- identifying various monetary values

ENGLISH LANGUAGE ARTS

- describing main and subsidiary characters
- most significant: works of an author, literary movements, or decades

- words or phrases indicating different intensities of feeling or situations (e.g., hungry, starving, peckish, filled to bursting, stuffed, satiated, filled up)

- evaluating scariest, happiest, or silliest books or films

- critiquing favorite or least favorite books or films

SOCIAL STUDIES

- sorting cities by population size (income generated, position from North to South, East to West)

- ranking the industries that contribute to the economy

- ranking the largest producers of a commodity in the world

SCIENCE

- ranking the size of planets to understand the effect of gravitational force

- compare the gestation periods, number of young produced, life expectancy of different animals to interpret the significance of reproduction characteristics in the survival of the species

- rank densities of different matter

- rank the most polluted cities in the USA, the world, etc. to clarify causes and effects of air quality

- rank different wind strengths to predict storm damage and the types of safety precautions that should be taken

LEARNING A LANGUAGE
(*English Language Learners or Learning a Foreign Language*)

- written numbers in the language

- most crucial vocabulary words for survival in another language

- words associated with measurement

- words related to size (e.g., short, shorter, shortest)

- ordinal words (first, second, third…)

PHYSICAL EDUCATION

- achievements of professional athletes
- world records
- personal performances
- number of players on a team
- forms of exercise according to how many calories are burned off

THE ARTS

- length of different musical notes
- different musical terms according to tempo or volume
- influences on a composer or artist
- shades of color
- levels of abstraction in art

TECHNOLOGY

- best museum sites on the Internet
- best places to buy things on the Internet
- technical equipment according to price (capacity, portability, response time)
- digital cameras according to number of pixels in the image
- effectiveness of different search engines

FREQUENTLY ASKED QUESTIONS ABOUT ORDERING

My students do not understand Ordering by Rank. What do I do?

Students usually understand Ordering by Time and Ordering by Occurrence. These are rather straightforward. However, the connection between the mental steps in the skill of Ordering by Rank may be less clear as students expect the significance of factors they study to be determined by the teacher or experts.

One reason that Ordering by Rank can be more difficult is there are times when the purpose and criteria for the ranking are subjective (for example, a list of favorite movies). Students must see that we can rank items any way we choose for any purpose we choose.

The following exercise is simple and illustrates the connection between the mental steps in Ordering by Rank.

Exercise:

Choose a few students to be the items for Ordering by Rank.

<u>Items</u>	<u>Purpose of Ranking</u>	<u>Criterion(a) for Ranking</u>
Students	To organize students from tallest to shortest	Height

Students may carry out the ranking of the items (students) by physically arranging the items according to the criterion. Then change the criterion for ranking to hair color instead of height, and have students rank the items. Students will better understand the connection of the steps in the mental skill.

On Solid Ground: Teaching the Structured Thinking Skill of Supporting a Conclusion in the Student-Centered Classroom

*Students are meaning-making sparks,
all on their own quests.*

—Bill Ayers

ON SOLID GROUND: TEACHING THE STRUCTURED THINKING SKILL OF SUPPORTING A CONCLUSION IN THE STUDENT-CENTERED CLASSROOM

12

In life, we draw conclusions constantly about things we encounter: the people we meet, the television programs we watch, the books we read, what we did yesterday, and so on.

We use the skill of Supporting a Conclusion in two ways:

- **Examining My Own Conclusion**
- **Examining an Author's Conclusion**

When someone asks us if we had a good vacation, we do not describe every detail. Instead, we may say that Greece is a great place for a summer vacation. It has a wonderful climate, many historical sites, good food, and warm and friendly people. Alternatively, we may explain that we had a rotten vacation. Our luggage was lost, our money was stolen, the hotel was dirty, and the flights were delayed.

Many advertisers target young people to push them to reach conclusions about what they are selling, whether it is a particular brand of sneaker, fast food, tomato ketchup, or cell phone.

Often students will reach a conclusion or agree with someone else's conclusion but not be able to explain their thinking. For example, they may say, "That new CD is wicked!" and when asked why say, "Well it just is."

Once students know the steps in this skill, they will be able to clearly lay out the support or reasons for their conclusions and examine the conclusions others are trying to persuade them to reach.

 POINTER: Recognize the benefits of Effective Group Process.

Because the rules of Effective Group Process create an environment in which everyone's contribution is valued, students feel comfortable sharing their conclusions and realize they benefit from hearing the conclusions of their classmates. As students practice writing conclusions and hearing those of others, their conclusions will become more sophisticated and refined.

THE STRUCTURED THINKING SKILL OF SUPPORTING A CONCLUSION ENABLES STUDENTS TO:

- formulate conclusions and articulate reasons or support for conclusions.

- identify the point of view of a written passage and give supporting reasons from the text.

- examine an author's conclusions and determine whether they are justifiable.

- examine speeches and prose in which the goal is to persuade the audience to believe or do something.

- develop a convincing argument.

- develop the confidence and ability to draw conclusions.

TEACHING THE STRUCTURED THINKING SKILL OF SUPPORTING A CONCLUSION TO EXAMINE AN AUTHOR'S CONCLUSION

Introducing the Skill
You can use the steps in Supporting a Conclusion to examine a conclusion that someone else is trying to convince you to believe. Bring in an advertisement for something that is appealing to students. Ask students to verbalize what they think the advertiser wants the consumer to believe. Ask students to list what the advertiser is using to support the conclusion. Finally, have them state a conclusion about the advertisement.

Ask students to think of other situations in which someone is trying to persuade them to believe something (e.g., campaign literature, an argument a friend might make to convince them to do something, etc.). Say that there are steps that you go through to examine conclusions and support that an author is advocating.

First Step In Skill
State the author's conclusion.
Have students read a pamphlet about the promotion of good dental care.

Sample conclusion for *Dental Care*:

> Dentists believe prevention is better than cure. Serious dental problems in later life can be prevented if parents start caring for their children's teeth at a young age.

Second Step In Skill
Find and list the support given in the text for this conclusion.

164

Sample response for *Dental Care*:

Conclusion			
Serious dental problems in later life can be prevented if parents start caring for their children's teeth at a young age.			
Support	**Support**	**Support**	**Support**
Parents must teach children how to brush their teeth using a different technique than adults because children's limited dexterity means that they cannot brush as an adult would. All surfaces of the teeth should be brushed with a circular motion.	Toothbrushes should be changed every three to four months, especially in the cold and flu season, when germs are more prevalent.	Children need to begin going to the dentist early, as soon as their first tooth appears.	Parents should clean a young baby's mouth with a baby washcloth or gauze to avoid the build up of plaque on the gums. The infant will be used to a plaque-free mouth and be more likely to clean his or her teeth later in life.

Third Step in Skill
Identify any unstated reasons or assumptions the author may be using to support the conclusion.

Sample response for *Dental Care*

People want to keep their teeth.
Good dental care helps preserve teeth.

Fourth Step in Skill
State an interpretation or summary regarding the author's conclusion and support.

Sample interpretation or summary for *Dental Care*:

There are many things that you can do early on to prevent dental problems in later life. These include regular trips to the dentist, establishing a regimen for cleaning your teeth at a young age and eating a healthy diet. Your beautiful smile can last a lifetime if you look after your teeth.

You can also use this skill with any text to break down the point of a written passage, to examine the author's intent e.g. in a persuasive essay. When learning the skill, work with a relatively short passage. Once students know the skill, they can use it with longer articles or more than one text.

First Step in Skill
State the author's conclusion.

Select a passage or article in which an author is putting forward a particular perspective of a situation. In this example, we use the text 'Of Revenge' by Francis Bacon. Either read the text aloud to students or have them read it individually. Ask them to complete the first step of the skill.

OF REVENGE
Francis Bacon
(First published in 1597)

REVENGE is a kind of wild justice; which the more man's nature runs to, the more ought law to weed it out. For as for the first wrong, it doth but offend the law; but the revenge of that wrong, putteth the law out of office. Certainly, in taking revenge, a man is but even with his enemy; but in passing it over, he is superior; for it is a prince's part to pardon. And Salomon, I am sure, saith, *It is the glory of a man to pass by an offence.* That which is past is gone, and irrevocable; and wise men have enough to do, with things present and to come; therefore they do but trifle with themselves, that labor in past matters. There is no man doth a wrong, for the wrong's sake; but thereby to purchase himself profit, or pleasure, or honor, or the like. Therefore, why should I be angry with a man, for loving himself better than me? And if any man should do wrong, merely out of ill-nature, why, yet it is but like the thorn or briar, which prick and scratch, because they can do no other. The most tolerable sort of revenge, is for those wrongs which there is no law to remedy; but then let a man take heed, the revenge be such as there is no law to punish; else a man's enemy is still before hand, and it is two for one. Some, when they take revenge, are desirous, the party should know, whence it cometh. This is the more generous. For the delight seemeth to be, not so much in doing the hurt, as in making the party repent. But base and crafty cowards, are like the arrow that flieth in the dark. Cosmus, duke of Florence, had a desperate saying against perfidious or neglecting friends, as if those wrongs were unpardonable; *You shall read* (saith he) *that we are commanded to forgive our enemies; but you never read, that we are commanded to forgive our friends.* But yet the spirit of Job was in a better tune: *Shall we* (saith he) *take good at God's hands, and not be content to take evil also?* And so of friends in a proportion. This is certain, that a man that studieth revenge, keeps his own wounds green, which otherwise would heal, and do well. Public revenges are for the most part fortunate; as that for the death of Cæsar; for the death of Pertinax; for the death of Henry the Third of France; and many more. But in private revenges, it is not so. Nay rather, vindictive persons live the life of witches; who, as they are mischievous, so end they infortunate.

Depending on their reading ability, read it aloud or have students read it to themselves. Have them write down the conclusion that the author wants you to believe in this passage.

Sample conclusion for 'Of Revenge:'

> A man that studieth revenge, keeps his own wounds green, which otherwise would heal, and do well.

Second Step In Skill
Find and list the support given in the text for this conclusion.
Ask students to refer back to the text and list all the support that the author gives to support the conclusion.

Sample response for 'Of Revenge:'

Conclusion
A man that studieth revenge, keeps his own wounds green, which otherwise would heal, and do well.
Support
Revenge is the kind of justice that law should weed out.
Revenge offends law itself.
Revenge puts the law out of office.
It is a prince's part to pardon.
Taking revenge puts man on an even level with the enemy.

Students can now share the support they found with each other, in pairs, with the large group, or in small groups. If they are reporting to the large group, ensure that they are sharing with each other and not reporting to you. They may ask each other to reference where in the text they found their information. This is fine.

Third Step In Skill
Identify any unstated reasons or assumptions the author may be using to support the conclusion.
Ask students to list anything that the author has assumed when writing this text. Use Group Process to allow students to share their ideas.

Sample response for 'Of Revenge:'

Unstated Or Assumed Reasons
Some people would disagree that wild justice is bad
Getting even with the enemy is not good

Fourth Step in Skill

State an interpretation or summary regarding the author's conclusion and support.

Ask students to write a summary about the author's conclusion. Let them share their ideas and then reflect on and refine what they have written.

Sample interpretation or summary for 'Of Revenge:'

> Francis Bacon believes that a person who takes revenge will not end his suffering but instead extend it and make it worse. In our society, those who commit a crime are punished by the law and not by individuals taking revenge.

**SUPPORTING A CONCLUSION:
EXAMINING AN AUTHOR'S CONCLUSION**

Directions for Elementary Students

Step One: What do you think is the author's conclusion?

Step Two: List all the reasons that you can find.

Step Three: What do you think about the author's conclusion?

**SUPPORTING A CONCLUSION:
EXAMINING AN AUTHOR'S CONCLUSION**

Directions for Secondary Students

Step One: State the author's conclusion.

Step Two: Find and list the support given in the text for this conclusion.

Step Three: Identify any unstated reasons or assumptions the author may be using to support the conclusion.

Step Four: State an interpretation or summary regarding the author's conclusion and support.

TEACHING THE STRUCTURED THINKING SKILL OF SUPPORTING A CONCLUSION TO EXAMINE MY OWN CONCLUSION

First Step in Skill

State a conclusion about what you have seen or read.

Read or tell students the story of Goldilocks and the Three Bears and ask students to write or verbalize a conclusion about Goldilocks. When first teaching the skill, choose a conclusion that is representative of the group, write it up, and say that they are going to think of ideas that they can use to support their conclusion.

Sample conclusion for Goldilocks:

> Goldilocks was a naughty girl who was lucky that the three bears did not gobble her up.

Second Step in Skill

Find and list the support given in the text for this conclusion.

Ask students to list anything from the story that supports the conclusion. Write up the ideas that they suggest.

 ➤ **POINTER**: Allow students to ask questions of each other.

Students may question each other why something is offered as support. Let them use Group Process to discuss and share their thinking.

Sample response for Goldilocks:

> Her mother told her not to play in the woods and she ignored her. She found a house in the woods and entered it without permission.
> She ate food that did not belong to her. She touched property that did not belong to her (the chairs and the beds). She damaged property belonging to others (baby bear's chair).
> If Goldilocks had not run away, the bears might have eaten her.

Third Step in Skill

Identify any unstated assumptions related to your support.

Ask students to list any assumptions that may underlie the support or the conclusion. For the Structured Thinking Skill of Supporting a Conclusion, the type of assumptions we examine are the ideas that we may be taking for granted and using to support the conclusion.

Sample response for Goldilocks:

Support	Assumptions
Her mother told her not to play in the woods and she ignored her. She found a house in the woods and entered it without permission.	Children should obey their parents.
She ate food that did not belong to her. She touched property that did not belong to her (the chairs and the beds). She damaged property belonging to others (baby bear's chair).	You should not take things that belong to other people or enter property without permission.
If Goldilocks had not run away, the bears might have eaten her.	Bears eat people.

Fourth Step in Skill

State an interpretation or summary regarding your conclusion and support.
Ask students to write or verbalize a summary about their conclusion. Let them share their ideas and then reflect on and refine what they have written or said.

Sample interpretation or summary for Goldilocks:

If Goldilocks had not ignored her mother and gone into the bear's house, then the story would not have been so interesting. Fairy tales usually have happy endings, so even if the bears had caught Goldilocks they probably would not have eaten her. In real life, bears do eat people.

SUPPORTING A CONCLUSION:
EXAMINING MY OWN CONCLUSION

Directions for Elementary Students

Step One: In a few sentences, say something about what you have seen or read.

Step Two: List your support for saying that.

Step Three: Say something about your conclusion.

**SUPPORTING A CONCLUSION:
EXAMINING MY OWN CONCLUSION**

<u>**Directions for Secondary Students**</u>

Step One: State a conclusion about what you have seen or read.

Step Two: Find and list the support given in the text for this conclusion.

Step Three: Identify any unstated assumptions related to your support.

Step Four: State an interpretation or summary regarding your conclusion and support.

INCORPORATING SUPPORTING A CONCLUSION INTO LESSONS

You can apply this skill to situations in which students have to advance a judgment and provide support. Through using the skill in conjunction with Effective Group Process, they will see that different people have different viewpoints. The important thing is that you can support your viewpoint with clear, accurate reasons or ideas.

You can use this skill to respond to any stimulus in a structured way (e.g., music, painting, sculpture, charts, or tables). Students can use it to create the outline of a persuasive essay or respond to a persuasive piece written by someone else.

You can use it as the main part of a lesson where students must produce a substantial piece of writing or as an introductory or closing activity when students respond to a short paragraph, a quotation, or chart.

SAMPLE SUPPORTING A CONCLUSION ACTIVITIES

MATHEMATICS

- interpret a chart or graph

- interpret a sequence of numbers (square, triangular, or Fibonacci)

- reach a conclusion about which statistical measure—mean, median, mode, or range—would be most suitable to use to interpret a selection of data

ENGLISH LANGUAGE ARTS

- find the "main idea" in a text

- determine the "author's intent" in a text

- respond to any text by determining a conclusion about what it says

- draw conclusions about particular characters in a story or the reasons that a character gives for a particular action

- plan for a debate

- analyze a persuasive argument

- examine the ideas put forward by different advertisers

SOCIAL STUDIES

- formulate conclusions regarding the actions of historical figures or the significance of particular historical events

- give reasons for taking particular actions during particular situations such as a hurricane, blizzard, earthquake, or flood

- provide reasons to back up controversial political, economic, or social opinions

- examine the reasons for citing a proposed construction project—shopping mall, airport, or nuclear power plant—in a particular place

- examine the reasons for people leaving their home countries

- evaluate the Declaration of Independence as a persuasive argument

- evaluate the reasons underlying colonialism

- evaluate the reasons for proposed foreign policy decisions

- evaluate the reasons for territorial expansion

- identify the reasons underlying important social movements

SCIENCE

- give reasons why people should eat a balanced meal

- give reasons why a particular conclusion has been formed following a scientific experiment

- provide reasons to support a controversial opinion in science

- examine reasons for protecting the environment

- examine reasons for immunizing young children against different diseases

FOREIGN LANGUAGE

- give reasons for studying a language

- find "main idea" in a text, conversation, etc. in a different language

- interpret the nuances of someone speaking in a different language based on cultural customs of communication

- examine instructions, foodstuffs, cleaning materials, etc. from a different country regarding health and safety

PHYSICAL EDUCATION

- state why everyone needs to be concerned about AIDS

- provide reasons for pursuing a particular exercise program

- examine the ideas behind different weight loss programs

THE ARTS

- respond to a piece of music or art

- give reasons supporting why you like a particular type of music or art

- examine what an artist is attempting to express through a particular piece of art or music

TECHNOLOGY

- articulate your conclusion regarding different products or applications

- examine companies' claims about their software or hardware

FREQUENTLY ASKED QUESTIONS ABOUT SUPPORTING A CONCLUSION

The first problem students have is that they do not know the difference between support and a conclusion. How do I get them to separate the two?

Let students create a definition for support and a definition for a conclusion. The creation of the definitions may take 30 to 40 minutes but the information they gain will be worth the time.

My students cannot recognize the support for a conclusion when they are reading a reference. What do I do?

Ask students to identify one supporting reason or idea at a time using only short passages of reference material. The amount of reading material will not intimidate them if the passage is short. With longer passages, they can consider the text a paragraph at a time. They will become comfortable with recognizing different supporting reasons and ideas if they do not have to consider the whole reference at one time. One benefit of this exercise is that students' reading levels will increase in a short period. They will focus on each part of the reference as they read it and they will not be distracted by the length of the material. This helps develop students' text comprehension skills.

My students identify only one supporting idea reason for a conclusion and then consider the exercise completed. How do I get them to realize that there is more than one supporting idea or reason related to a conclusion?

State a conclusion for which you *know* students will be able to find support. Use a conclusion such as, "The school board should not agree with the proposal that all students in our school system wear school uniforms." Students will supply a list of ideas or reasons that support the conclusion. Then ask students if they believe that only *one* of the ideas or reasons would be enough to convince the school board that they should not vote for the proposal. Students will understand that there is strength in amount of support for a conclusion. It is also beneficial to have students determine which of the supporting ideas or reasons is the most important, and to list the other supporting ideas or reasons in order of importance and share them with the group. They will see that individuals may have different priorities.

13

Lesson and Unit Planning

*It's not what is poured into a student that counts,
but what is planted.*

—Linda Conway

LESSON AND UNIT PLANNING

13

You will find that you can teach much of your curriculum content using one of the Ventures Initiative and Focus® Strategies. Because each of the strategies gives students the opportunity to process the content for themselves, simply applying them to your curriculum will assist you in making the shift to a student-centered classroom.

Students easily learn these strategies, so you can begin using them immediately. As a facilitator of student learning, you will make sure that students stay in their Thinking Aloud Paired Problem Solving (TAPPS) roles, adhere to the rules of Effective Group Process, and work through the steps in the Structured Thinking Skills. You will also be providing the resources that students need to complete their work.

 **POINTERS**

> **Start with TAPPS.**
> The simplest way to begin is by developing TAPPS exercises. You can incorporate TAPPS into any content numerous times during the day.
>
> You can plan a TAPPS activity as an introduction, a wrap-up, and/or during the main body of a lesson. You may even incorporate TAPPS several times during one lesson.

> **Use the Effective Group Process Discussion Process.**
> Create a schedule of lessons (see the section entitled "Creating an Implementation Schedule for Introducing the Skills and Techniques") to formally teach Group Process using the Effective Group Process Discussion guidelines. In other lessons, have students practice using Group Process while sharing information.

 POINTERS: Give students ownership of "the answer."

> **Start with Examining Similarities and Differences.**
> Although you can probably choose any of the Structured Thinking Skills and be successful, we have found that it is best to begin with the skill of Examining Similarities and Differences. Students are usually familiar with the idea of finding similarities and differences, but they are usually unaware of the additional mental steps that they go through to reach an interpretation or summary statement.

Examining Similarities and Differences uncovers what we do naturally and automatically and clearly demonstrates that Structured Thinking Skills have specific mental steps. Once they become aware of the steps in a type of thinking, students can start to become systematic thinkers.

➤ **Use one skill at a time.**

When you begin to teach the Structured Thinking Skills, you will probably use only one skill during a lesson. Later, as you and your students become more confident in the steps, you will find that you will incorporate several of the strategies into one lesson.

➤ **Use different skills with the same content.**

Even though at the beginning you will only be using one skill per lesson, you can revisit the same curriculum content in subsequent lessons with a different skill. Students will not learn everything that they need to know about a subject by doing one TAPPS or one Structured Thinking Skill. Every time they revisit the subject, students will gain a greater understanding of the content. For example, students may first study the human digestive system by Analyzing the Parts of a Whole, followed by Ordering by Occurrence the functions that the different organs perform in the human digestive process, and then Grouping and Categorizing the different organs. With each subsequent activity, students become more familiar with the information. They will also be able to retain and apply the content in a far more effective way than if they had learned it using traditional teacher-centered methods like lecture or rote memorization.

 POINTERS

➤ **Use the skills to teach the skills.**

You can use Structured Thinking Skills to develop students' understanding of the various strategies. For example:

- Analyzing the Parts of a Whole to examine the rules of Effective Group Process

- Examining Similarities and Differences between your classroom rules and the rules of Effective Group Process

- Examining Similarities and Differences between the role of the Listener and the role of the Problem Solver in TAPPS

- Examining Similarities and Differences between an Effective Group Process discussion and another type of group discussion

- Analyzing the Parts of a Whole of the steps in a Structured Thinking Skill

- Examining Similarities and Differences between two Structured Thinking Skills

- Ordering by Occurrence the steps in TAPPS, an Effective Group Process discussion, or a Structured Thinking Skill

> ➤ Give it time.
>
> Each of the strategies may not work perfectly the first time. Over time, through practice, students do get better at thinking, articulating their thinking, and working in a group.

CHOOSING A SKILL OR TECHNIQUE FOR YOUR LESSON PLANS

BASIC VENTURES INITIATIVE AND FOCUS® STRATEGIES	

Constructive Communication Techniques
 	
• TAPPS
 	
• Effective Group Process Discussion
	Basic Structured Thinking Skills
	
	• Defining and Describing
	
	• Examining Similarities and Differences
	
	• Analyzing the Parts of a Whole
	
	• Categorizing and Grouping
	
	• Ordering by:
	  - Time
	  - Occurrence
	  - Rank
	
	• Supporting a Conclusion

Define Student Outcomes

When planning a lesson, examine your expected student outcomes—what students must know or be able to do—and select one of the strategies from the list of Basic Ventures Initiative and Focus® Strategies. If students must be able to interpret a graph, they could use Analyzing the Parts of a Whole to examine the different aspects of a graph. If they must distinguish between simile and metaphor, they could use Examining Similarities and Differences. If they need to place the stages of ecological succession in order, they could use Ordering by Occurrence.

Assess Students' Entry Level

Remember that the strategies are a tool for delivering curriculum content. The one that you use will depend both on the nature of the content and students' level of entry into that content. All of the strategies that you are learning are basic ones used to develop clarification and understanding of information that is new to the learner. There is no one best skill for student mastery of content. Do not think that you *must* use a particular skill.

Look at the Content

Identify a thinking skill that students could use to process whatever content they are investigating. Remember that there will be more than one skill that students could use, so choose the one that seems to fit student outcomes the best. Most times, students could learn the same content using any of the skills. The more students interact with the information the greater their understanding will be. Just remember to allow students to do their own thinking.

THE VESC™ LESSON PLAN

The VESC™ lesson plan is a guide to writing lessons that incorporates the VESC™ skills and techniques. Because many of its components are universal, you can easily adapt it to fit the requirements of your school or district. What may be different are the components that focus on student **communication** and **mental processing**.

Many schools compile the VESC™ lessons that their teachers write into a booklet for all teachers to use. These lessons also contribute to a body of evidence that the school can compile to show what the school is doing to raise the levels of achievement.

The following is the annotated lesson plan to use as a guide as you write your own lessons. You will find a blank template in Appendix C, "Classroom Integration of VESC™ Strategies."

SCHOOL	The name of your school
NAME	Your name
SUBJECT	The subject area addressed
CONTENT	The content area addressed
GRADE LEVEL	Grade levels of students
STANDARDS ADDRESSED	The Strategy and Topic, *e.g., Examining Similarities and Differences between Buddhism and Christianity.*
ASSESSMENT	The type of assessment, *e.g., oral presentation with a poster of the graphic organization of the facts.*
HOMEWORK	The activities students will complete following the lesson, *e.g., identify present controversies based on religious beliefs. Gather information from a variety of media. Summarize information from each source.*
LESSON	The lesson elements, *e.g., describe how you will activate prior knowledge, how students will engage the main activities of the lesson, and how you will bring the lesson to closure. Be specific about the strategies you will use, student groupings, mode of instruction, and communication techniques.*

When you plan your lessons, choose the Structured Thinking Strategies that are the best match to the content. Ensure that students participate in the thinking process by allowing for student-to-student discussion. Vary your mode of instruction by scheduling time for students to work alone, with a partner, in a small group, or as part of a whole class. Finally, ensure that at the end of a lesson, students have the opportunity to reflect individually on content and come to their own conclusions.

CREATING AN IMPLEMENTATION SCHEDULE FOR INTRODUCING THE VENTURES INITIATIVE AND FOCUS® STRATEGIES

Every curriculum contains a vast amount of information and ideas that students must master. The introduction of the Ventures Initiative and Focus® Strategies will not compromise this goal. In fact, we have found that once students have learned the techniques, they are able to learn the content quicker and more effectively than when more traditional methods are used. In addition, because the VESC™ system is designed to work with any curriculum, you can easily integrate your curriculum and the strategies and use the resources you already have.

As we discussed earlier, we recommend introducing TAPPS and Effective Group Process followed by the thinking skill of Examining Similarities and Differences. Once you have laid this groundwork, you can introduce additional Structured Thinking Skills every other week or so.

Remember that when you teach the skill you are going to use some very simple content that allows students to focus on the mental steps of the process. After this introduction to the skill, students can practice it using appropriate curriculum content.

The following is a sample implementation schedule. It demonstrates how you would have students learn a new skill while they continue to practice the ones you have introduced. There is also a blank template for you to photocopy and use in Appendix C, "Classroom Integration of VESC™ Strategies."

You will base the implementation schedule you create on your students and your curriculum. For example, younger students work more with Categorizing and Grouping than Supporting a Conclusion. You may also choose a different order of skills depending on the content students must master.

SUGGESTED IMPLEMENTATION SCHEDULE

WEEK	NEW VESC™ STRATEGIES PRESENTED IN TEACHER WORKSHOPS	CLASSROOM INTRODUCTION OF VESC™ STRATEGIES	CLASSROOM PRACTICE OF VESC™ STRATEGIES
3	Examining Similarities and Differences	TAPPS Effective Group Process	TAPPS Effective Group Process
4		Examining Similarities and Differences	TAPPS Effective Group Process Discussion
5	Analyzing the Parts of a Whole		TAPPS Effective Group Process Discussion Examining Similarities and Differences
6		Analyzing the Parts of a Whole	TAPPS Effective Group Process Discussion Examining Similarities and Differences
7	Ordering by Time		TAPPS Effective Group Process Discussion Examining Similarities and Differences Analyzing the Parts of a Whole

UNIT PLANNING

Introduction

Once students have been introduced to the Basic Strategies and have had a sufficient opportunity to practice them, the next step is incorporating them into a larger unit of study. Once you know the Basic Strategies, you may actually find it easier to incorporate them across a unit rather than in isolated lessons.

MAKE CONTENT CONNECTIONS

Through unit planning and creating a sequence of lessons, you can build content connections. Revisiting the same content using different strategies allows students to build their learning on what has gone before. As they make associations between what they learn in the different lessons, they continually develop their understanding of the topic and learn to apply what they know to new situations.

THINK THEMATICALLY

When we plan units using large chunks of the curriculum, it is easier to think thematically. Immersion in a theme engages students over a longer period. Students learn relationships and construct an understanding of the larger and bigger ideas rather than memorizing individual facts. In the end, students achieve a higher level of understanding of the topic.

MAKE SKILL AND TECHNIQUE CONNECTIONS

As you begin to plan units, you will also see how the different strategies are connected and how powerful they are when they work together. It takes time to get to this point, so remember that there are many ways of using them.

DIFFERENTIATE

The design of the unit allows for individual instruction for students who are at different levels of understanding of the content topics. The self-assessment sheet in the next section will help you plan what skills you can use differently for students in your class.

PLAN LONG TERM

On a practical level, unit planning provides structure to teaching. You know what you will be doing for a large chunk of time. By taking a more global view of your curriculum, you will be able to prepare a collection of integrated lessons.

How to Prepare a Unit Plan

The specific length of the unit and its nature will vary depending on the school, district, or state in which you teach. To prepare for the beginning of the unit, review your curriculum and ensure that it is aligned with state standards. To do this, look at the state standards and list those that you will address through the teaching of the unit. Then consider whether you must make any adaptations to address additional relevant standards.

As you have done with individual lessons, you will now look at this larger body of curriculum content and decide which of the strategies you could use to deliver the content in a student-centered way. You will plan activities and products such as class work, homework, and long-term assignments.

Plan a variety of assignments that students will produce and different types of activities for them to engage in (essays, charts, oral presentations, models, dramatizations, etc.). Students should have multiple ways in which to demonstrate their understanding of the content. The beauty of going through this exercise is that you create a resource that you or colleagues can use with future classes. You will find an empty template in Appendix C, "Classroom Integration of VESC™ Strategies," to duplicate and use for your unit planning. The following is a VESC™ Annotated Unit Plan.

VESC™ ANNOTATED UNIT PLAN

Subject Area: Write the subject area here, e.g., math, science, visual arts
Content Unit: Write the name of the unit that is being studied, e.g., the Impressionists, the geometry of triangles

Standards: Write the standards that students will address during this unit. Think about standards across the curriculum. Every unit will address some of the reading and writing standards, as students will engage in these activities within the subject area.

CONTENT OBJECTIVES (Students will be able to…)	TYPE OF THINKING NEEDED TO RESPOND	LESSON USING VESC™ STRATEGIES AND CONTENT SPECIFICS	STUDENT PRODUCTS AND ACTIVITIES
In this column, write *all* the content objectives that students will learn when they study this topic.	In this column, record the type of thinking that students will engage in, e.g., Grouping, Examining Similarities and Differences, etc.	In this column, write the specific Structured Thinking Skills students will use and the specific content they will process, e.g., Grouping and Categorizing different types of triangles, Examining Similarities and Differences between acute and obtuse triangles.	In this column, describe the work that students will produce, e.g., a chart Examining Similarities and Differences between obtuse and acute triangles.
Unit Resources and Technology Integration			
List all the materials that you need to gather that relate to the unit, e.g., postcard packs, slides, books, videos, and a list of Internet sites. You could organize these into resource packs to use again when you repeat the unit.			

UNIT PLANNING EXAMPLE: IMPRESSIONISM

Listed below are the content objectives from a typical art curriculum unit plan. Students will study these areas as part of a unit on Impressionism.

As part of the unit, students will:

- describe the work of the Impressionist artists.
- examine the development of Impressionist art.
- emulate the work of Impressionist artists.
- analyze the use of color, texture, and tone.
- study the work of two of the following: Sisley, Degas, Pissarro, Van Gogh, Monet, Renoir.

As you can see, there is no mention of the *ways* that students will address the content. In fact, there is no guarantee that students will be doing any of the processing. Instead, the teacher could provide a series of lectures or worksheets that do not require students to think at all.

If we were to think about how we would teach this as part of a VESC™ student-centered classroom, we would address the same content but we would also be explicit about how students are going to think about and interact with the information.

When they are studying this unit, students will:

- use Defining to identify the key characteristics of the Impressionist movement
- use Describing to identify the key characteristics of an Impressionist painting
- use the skill of Categorizing to sort examples of works by Sisley, Degas, Pissarro, Van Gogh, Monet, and Renoir
- Ordering by Time the major events that had an impact on the Impressionist movement
- Ordering by Time the works of a range of Impressionist artists
- Ordering by Rank to determine the most significant works of the Impressionist movement
- Ordering by Time the works of one of the artists listed and use the skill of Sequencing by Rank to identify the artist's most significant works
- Examining Similarities and Differences between a work by Degas and a work by Monet (or any other two Impressionist artists)
- use Categorizing and/or Grouping to sort Impressionist works according to their color, texture, and tone
- use Analyzing the Parts of a Whole to examine works from the Impressionist movement and use what was learned to create paintings in a similar style

The following sample unit plan on Impressionism shows how you can implement this unit.

SAMPLE UNIT PLAN: IMPRESSIONISM

Performing Arts/Art			**Content Unit:** Impressionism
National Art Education Standards			
• Students should be able to develop and present basic analyses of works of art.			
• Students have an informed acquaintance with exemplary works from a variety of cultures and historical periods.			
• Students should be able to relate various types of arts knowledge and skills within and across artistic disciplines. This includes mixing and matching competencies and understandings in art history, and culture, and analysis in any arts-related project.			
National English Language Arts Standards			
• Students produce a narrative on a procedure.			
• Students read and comprehend informational materials to develop understanding and expertise to produce written or oral work.			
Content Objectives	**Type of Thinking**	**Lesson Using VESC™ Skill/Technique and Content Specifics**	**Student Products and Activities**
Describe the work of the Impressionist artists	**Defining and Describing** **Categorizing and Grouping** **Ordering**	Use **Defining and Describing** to identify the key characteristics of an Impressionist painting Use **Categorizing or Grouping** to group examples of works by Sisley, Degas, Pissarro, Van Gogh, Monet, Renoir **Ordering by Time** the works of a range of Impressionist artists	Students write a paragraph that will introduce someone to a collection of Impressionist paintings Students sort the works according to the artist and identify any recurring themes Students create a timeline
Examine the development of Impressionist art	**Ordering**	**Ordering by Time** the major events that had an impact on the Impressionist movement and **Ordering by Rank** to determine the most significant works	Students create a parallel timeline that depicts what was happening in the areas in which the Impressionists lived and worked
Emulate the work of Impressionist artists	**Analyzing the Parts of a Whole**	Use **Analyzing the Parts of a Whole** to examine a number of works from the Impressionist movement and create a painting in a similar style	Students create a piece of art in the Impressionist style
Analyze the use of color, texture, and tone	**Grouping and Categorizing**	Use **Grouping and Categorizing** to sort Impressionist works according to their color, texture, and tone	Students create a web from their grouping chart to produce a guide to determine whether a piece of work is an Impressionist work
Study the work of an Impressionist painter	**Ordering**	**Ordering by Time** the works of one of the above artists **Ordering by Rank** the artist's most significant works	Students write an illustrated biography of the Impressionist artist of their choice
Study the work of an Impressionist and Neo-Impressionist artist	**Defining and Describing**	Use **Defining and Describing** to identify the key characteristics of Impressionism and Neo-Impressionism art	Students create a booklet that could be a museum guide on an Impressionist and Neo-Impressionist artist
	Examining Similarities and Differences	**Examining Similarities and Differences** between Impressionism and Neo-Impressionism **Examining Similarities and Differences** between an Impressionist and Neo-Impressionist artist	
Unit Resources and Technology Integration			
Books on the Impressionist movement; postcards of examples of works; Explore Internet sites, e.g., Metropolitan Museum of Art, New York; Museé D'Orsay, Paris; Giverney, France; Paints, oil pastels, soft art pencils and watercolors			

The following unit plan shows how this format can be applied to a science curriculum.

SAMPLE UNIT PLAN: CELLS

Life Science/Biology			Content Unit: Cells
National Science Education Standards • Content Standard A: As a result of activities, all students should develop abilities necessary to do scientific inquiry and understandings about scientific inquiry. • Content Standard C: As a result of activities, all students should develop understanding of the cell			
Content Objectives: Students will be able to:	**Type of Thinking Needed to Respond**	**Lesson Using VESC™ Strategies and Content Specifics**	**Student Products and Activities**
Discuss several theories about how life was formed	**Categorizing** and **Grouping** **Ordering**	**Grouping** and **Categorizing** of life formation theories **Ordering by Occurrence** the life formation theories	Oral presentation of theories done in pairs and whole-class Students will use their notes to write a descriptive essay
Identify basic characteristics	**Grouping**	**Categorizing** and **Grouping** of living and nonliving objects	Students will create a poster of classification criteria
Describe metabolism	**Categorizing** **Ordering**	**Categorizing** the types of metabolism **Ordering by Occurrence** the types of metabolism	Students will create a chart of the information
Identify the basic needs of living things	**Analyzing the Parts of a Whole**	**Analyzing the Parts of a Whole** of the needs of living things	Students will write a descriptive essay
Define "homeostasis"	**Defining**	Students will use **Defining**	Students will verbalize definitions using Group Process
Distinguish between elements and compounds	**Examining Similarities and Differences** **Analyzing the Parts of a Whole**	**Examining Similarities and Differences** between elements and compounds **Analyzing the Parts of a Whole** of the elements and the compounds	Students will make notes and give an oral presentation Students will produce a written description that includes a diagram
Describe the organic compounds that are the building blocks of life	**Describing** **Categorizing**	**Describing** each of the compounds **Categorizing** of each of the compounds	Students will write a descriptive essay Students present their Grouping Charts
Discuss the historical development of cell theory	**Describing** **Ordering**	**Describing** the present-day cell theory **Ordering by Time** the steps that led to the development of the present-day cell theory	Students will give an oral presentation Students will write a descriptive essay relating the development of the present-day cell theory
Describe the structure of a cell Identify functions of the parts of the cell	**Analyzing the Parts of a Whole**	**Analyzing the Parts of a Whole** of the cell	Students will view prepared slides of plant and animal cells Students will create and label a clay model and give an oral presentation
Describe the five levels of organization of living things	**Ordering**	**Ordering by Rank** the steps in the organization of cells in a multi-cellular organism	Students will create a flow chart designed to illustrate the steps in the organization of cells
Unit Resources and Technology Integration			
Textbook: Pages 47-68, Film: *Life on Earth,* Internet sites: Cells Alive, Science Net, Eureka Science, CD ROM and film clips of cells, Microscope slides, Charts and posters of slides			

Student Assessment

The Ventures Initiative and Focus® Strategies will become an integral part of your student assessment practice. The work students produce while using them will form part of their grade. You will also assess student performance based on the specific rules or steps in each of the strategies.

USE MULTIPLE OPPORTUNITIES FOR FEEDBACK

Using these guidelines gives you the opportunity to give feedback at every stage and to grade individual students at different stages of the learning process. For example, a student may be writing an essay examining the similarities and differences between the work and lives of two authors. The first draft that the student submits may not contain enough details about the lives of the two authors. You could then direct the student to a resource so he or she can look for more similarities and differences between the lives of the two authors. This helps the student develop his or her work. This type of explicit feedback based on the guidelines does not make the student feel that the work done so far was of poor quality or a waste of time.

INVOLVE STUDENTS IN FREQUENT SELF-ASSESSMENT

Students will also be continually involved in the assessment process. As part of the lesson plan, students consider the thinking and communication skills they used and assess themselves using the guidelines.

Once students are comfortable with Defining and Describing, Categorizing and Grouping, Examining Similarities and Differences, Analyzing the Parts of a Whole, and Ordering, you can use two simple student self-assessment tools (see the text that follows). Students ask and answer the following questions:

- Can I define and describe the topic? (Defining and Describing)

- Can I group the topic into categories? (Categorizing and Grouping)

- Can I divide the topic into parts and verbalize the function of each part? (Analyzing the Parts of a Whole)

- Can I order any processes that relate to the topic? (Ordering by Time, by Rank, or Occurrence)

- Can I compare and contrast items related to the topic? (Examining Similarities and Differences)

Students use the "Student Prior Knowledge Self-Assessment" to determine their understanding of a topic at the beginning of a unit. Then, they will work on the unit using the Structured Thinking Skills to develop their understanding of the content. At the end of the unit, they complete a second self-assessment sheet, "Student End-of-Unit Self-Assessment Activities" to demonstrate their understanding of the topic. (Blank copies of these assessments are located in Appendix C, "Classroom Integration of VESC™ Strategies.")

The following is an example of a typical student response.

STUDENT PRIOR KNOWLEDGE SELF-ASSESSMENT

CONTENT UNIT: Mathematics, the circle

QUESTIONS TO ASK YOURSELF	YES	NO
Can I define and describe the topic?	A two-dimensional shape with no straight sides	
Can I group the topic into categories?	Area of the circle Different words associated with the circle, e.g., center, diameter radius, pi (π), circumference	
Can I divide the topic into parts and verbalize the function of each part?	Center Diameter Radius Circumference	
Can I order any processes that relate to the topic?		X
Can I examine similarities and differences between items related to the topic?	Circle and other two-dimensional shapes Circle and a sphere or cylinder	

Which Structured Thinking Skills could I use to learn more about this topic?

Examining Similarities and Differences

Ordering by Occurrence

Analyzing the Parts of a Whole

Grouping and Categorizing

STUDENT END-OF-UNIT SELF-ASSESSMENT ACTIVITIES

CONTENT UNIT:	Mathematics, the circle
Define and describe the topic	A circle is a closed-plane curve. Every point is the same distance from the center.
Group the topic into categories	Lines associated with the circle, e.g., circumference, radius, diameter, chord
	Portions of a circle, e.g., segments, sectors, semicircle
	The number π (pi)
	Finding the area of a circle
	Finding the circumference of a circle
Divide the topic into parts and verbalize the function of each part	The circumference is the boundary of the circle.
	The chord is the straight-line segment connecting two points on the circumference and the enclosed area.
	The diameter is the straight line that passes through the center of the circle.
Order any processes that relate to the topic	The diameter of any circle fits into the circumference 3.14 times. This is a special number called pi (π).
	To work out the circumference or area of a circle you use the ratio pi.
	To work out the circumference of a circle you use the formula $2\pi r$.
	To work out the area of a circle you use πr^2.
Examine Similarities and Differences of items related to the topic	Circle and other two-dimensional shapes
	Circle and a sphere or cylinder
	Finding the area of different circles and other polygons
	Finding the circumference of circles and the perimeters of other polygons
Which Structured Thinking Skills did I use to understand this topic?	
Analyzing the Parts of a Whole Categorizing and Grouping Examining Similarities and Differences Ordering by Occurrence	

 **POINTERS**

> ➢ Grade each step in the process to demonstrate that the working draft is valued as much as the finished product. Set specific deadlines that students are required to meet. Then, as students submit work, provide feedback on what they have completed so far.

> ➢ Give feedback to students promptly. Comment on student assignments in a way that is meaningful and will add to their understanding.

> ➢ Ensure that students know when and how the work is going to be graded.

> ➢ Ask students to assess their interactions and the work that they do.

> ➢ Continually assess what students have learned.

> ➢ Ensure that you plan regular review activities so concepts stay fresh in students' minds.

SAMPLE UNIT PLANS

THE LIFE OF FREDERICK DOUGLASS

- Ordering by Time the events according to when they happened

- Ordering by Occurrence how one event led to another

- Ordering by Rank the most significant events in the abolition of slavery

- Use Analyzing the Parts of a Whole to distinguish the different stages of Douglass' life

- Categorizing and Grouping to organize the main activities of his life

- Examining Similarities and Differences between his life with that of another person, (e.g., Abraham Lincoln)

PLACE VALUE

- Ordering by Rank ones, tens, hundreds, thousands, tens of thousands, hundreds of thousands, and millions

- Examining Similarities and Differences between the 4 in the number 14 with the 4 in the number 640,300

- Ordering by Rank a series of numbers

- Use Analyzing the Parts of a Whole on a range of large numbers

- Ordering by Occurrence the steps in performing the operations of addition, subtraction, multiplication, and division of numbers

- Examining Similarities and Differences between the original number and the number after the operation has been performed

- Use Supporting a Conclusion to examine the reasons for using each of the operations

AUTHOR STUDY

- Ordering by Time the author's works

- Ordering by Rank the author's most important works

- Use Categorizing and Grouping to organize the author's works

- Use Supporting a Conclusion to determine the influences on an author's work

- Examining Similarities and Differences between different works by the author

- Use Analyzing the Parts of a Whole to examine the plot, characters, setting, theme and conflict in different texts

Classroom Management: Student Engagement and Student Behavior

The secret of education is respecting the pupil.

—Ralph Waldo Emerson

CLASSROOM MANAGEMENT: STUDENT ENGAGEMENT AND STUDENT BEHAVIOR

14

Students are more likely to engage actively in classroom activities when the academic demands are neither too challenging nor too easy. When students are bored and uninterested or frustrated and fearful, they may behave in ways that disrupt learning for all the students. In these classrooms, the focus soon becomes the management of student behavior as opposed to student learning.

The strength of the VESC™ strategies and skills is that they are so simple to learn that every student is able use them. Indeed, with practice, students become very competent in their use. Further, the VESC™ system creates an environment with the expectation that all students will participate in the learning activities.

In VESC™ classrooms, students practice Thinking Aloud Paired Problem Solving (TAPPS), Effective Group Process, and the Structured Thinking Skills to engage in the mental processing of the curriculum content. These techniques allow students to move away from the arena in which they just memorize facts that they later forget. Instead, students process the material in ways that make it relevant and meaningful to them. When everyone in the classroom is involved and making meaningful connections to the curriculum, disruptions are few.

ESTABLISHING A CLASSROOM ENVIRONMENT

In most classrooms, the year begins with the establishment of rules geared toward managing student behavior. VESC™ classrooms also include guidelines for Constructive Communication that not only address student behavior, but also assist in establishing the conditions that allow students to become more involved in the learning process.

Once these guidelines are an established routine, students begin to feel comfortable admitting what they do not know and seek clarification when something is not clear. They begin to develop strategies they can use to stop them from shutting down when they face a challenging task. Students become more self-confident and far less reliant on praise and direction from the teacher.

Differentiation

These techniques also allow for true differentiation of outcome. Students process the curriculum content at their current level of understanding. Every student can participate in a TAPPS exercise, a Group Process discussion, or a Structured Thinking Skill regardless of his or her stage of learning.

Students also listen and learn from each other as they go through the process.

> For example, when asked to compare and contrast two pieces of music, students who know the steps in the Structured Thinking Skill of Examining Similarities and Differences can do it easily. Their responses will reflect what they know about music. One student may refer to a difference as speed and describe one piece as fast and the other as slow. Another student with more knowledge may refer to the same difference as tempo and make reference to the musical terms "allegro" and "andante." This is fine. The student who did not know the terms has now been exposed to them and may choose to include them in his or her notes. The teacher may decide that all the students need to know the musical terms associated with tempo and develop and use an Ordering by Rank exercise to teach them the terms.

The entire VESC™ approach is designed to give students the skills they need to be independent learners and achieve academic success. Once students experience success using these techniques, they recognize their value as tools that help them learn.

As the students become aware of their own learning, they also see how they learn from others and the benefit they gain from working in a group. Real group work happens. Real engagement develops.

TEACHER AND STUDENT ROLES

The roles of the teacher and students in VESC™ classrooms are different from those in classrooms that are more traditional. The VESC™ Classroom description that follows identifies the behavioral expectations for the teacher and student for each of the VESC™ strategies. Use it with your students to make explicit the learning and teaching behaviors that are expected in a VESC™ classroom.

THE VESC™ CLASSROOM

Teacher's Role	Student's Role
TALKING ALOUD PAIRED PROBLEM SOLVING	
• provide the guidelines for effective verbalization of thinking • provide the guidelines for effective listening • demonstrate how to separate my thinking from the thinking of the Problem Solver • assess each student	• practice speaking coherently whenever I am in the classroom • practice active listening • ask questions when I do not understand the Problem Solver • practice separating my thinking from the thinking of the Problem Solver • assess my ability to verbalize thinking
EFFECTIVE GROUP PROCESS	
• provide the guidelines for Effective Group Process • schedule practice sessions to learn Effective Group Process • expect the rules of Effective Group Process to be practiced by all students in the classroom • expect each student to self-correct behavior	• practice the guidelines of Effective Group Process daily • self-correct my behavior when I forget the guidelines of Effective Group Process • self-correct my behavior without disrupting the learning process • enter into the practice sessions for learning Effective Group Process • assess my ability to engage in Effective Group Process
STRUCTURED THINKING	
• raise my awareness of the type of thinking I am to use in the activity • teach the mental steps to use when using the Structured Thinking Skill • provide reference information to use • facilitate my use of the thinking skill • clarify reference information I do not understand	• become aware of my thinking • learn the mental steps I use to independently organize the information • use reference information to identify facts • organize facts according to the mental steps • assess facts for meaning • communicate the meaning of information • clarify information as I progress through the mental steps • ask questions when I do not understand

The Role of the Teacher

In the student-centered classroom, the student is the center of attention and activity. The teacher's role is that of a facilitator or mental coach and, occasionally, an information resource. The teacher does the following:

- Presents students with the material that they are going to learn (in the form of a text, diagram, video, picture, or object)

- Presents the skill that they are going use to process or organize this information

- When teaching a new strategy, takes students through the sequence of steps needed to complete it successfully

- Coaches students through the mental steps that they need to go through to complete the Structured Thinking Skill

- Allows students to process the content using the steps in the thinking skill (making notes and sharing using Effective Group Process at the appropriate intervals)

- Posts the steps or graphic organizer on the board or in chart form for student reference

- Writes student responses on a chalkboard or chart paper

- Ensures students are following the rules of Effective Group Process

- Has students review the steps in the skill or rules of the technique using the TAPPS process

Remember that the first few times students perform a skill they may not perform every step fully. Do not become frustrated and do not get involved directing the content, as this could shut down students' thinking. Your job is to coach students in the mental steps of the different Structured Thinking Skills and the rules for TAPPS and Effective Group Process. When we are learning something new we very rarely do something perfect the first few times. (Think back to when you learned to ride a bike or use a computer.) Mastery of the skill will come with practice.

THE FOCUS ON THINKING IN THE VESC™ CLASSROOM

One goal of a VESC™ student-centered classroom is to have students *thinking* most of the time. This may be a new experience for students. With this new focus on mental processing, they no longer simply memorize facts or engage in exercises in which they are able to get a good grade but actually have little understanding of what they have learned. For example, students often complete textbook exercises in which they can answer the questions without really knowing the content. Because they have not had to think about this new information, they will probably not be able to apply it to a new situation.

You can demonstrate this to the students by having them complete the Molek Siolus exercise. The words used in the exercise are "nonsense words." This allows students to focus on their mental processing as opposed to the content. Have students complete this or a similar exercise and use Group Process to discuss what they did. Generally, this exercise is only applicable to older students who are often asked to read texts and answer questions pertaining to what they read.

Directions: Read the following paragraph and answer the questions using complete sentences for your answers.

MOLEK SIOLUS

Because the molek siolus fract controls sactions that involve coctrans, warkes, and oplors, it has been compared to a niosulsus. The circuits of the niosulsus are located throughout the rihfrule. From the moment the niosulsus is manufactured, it is capable of controlling larehs, which are similar to sactions. Since the molek siolus fract controls sactions, which are the major cause of fuhlops, a disruption in the manufacture of the molek siolus fract could be hazardous to puelhs.

1. What does the molek siolus fract control?

2. To what has the molek siolus fract been compared?

3. Where are the circuits of the niosulsus located?

4. The larehs are similar to what other structures?

5. Predict the effect of a disruption in the manufacture of the molek siolus fract.

Introducing the Activity

Give them the reading passage and explain that it contains some information and some questions. Have them read the paragraph and answer the questions in complete sentences.

Follow-Up to the Activity

Ask students to think about the mental steps they used to answer the questions. Engage the students in a Group Process Discussion of the experience.

Typical student responses include:

- "I just knew the answers but I don't know how I know them."

- "It was easy once I realized they were nonsense words."

- "I could memorize the answers and use the information to answer the same questions on a test."

- "I completed the questions, but I still don't 'understand' the topic."

- "I've done things just like this before."

- "I don't know what 'mental steps' means."

This activity is significant for students because it clarifies the following:

- Activities like this require a minimal amount of effort.

- The activity does not accomplish an "understanding" of the topic.

- The format of the lesson is quite familiar: Give information and ask questions.

- They completed the exercise immediately using "strategies" they had developed yet were unaware of.

- They could even do well on a test of the information if the questions did not change much.

- They were uncomfortable slowing our thinking down to identify specific mental steps in completing the activity.

- They were uncomfortable in the verbalization of the mental steps.

In contrast, the introduction of the VESC™ strategies makes the student aware of the mental steps he or she uses when learning. Knowing how we learn provides a frame of reference for talking about mental processing and the factors that affect it. Over time, students become very skilled at articulating their thinking and managing themselves as learners.

PROCEDURES AND ROUTINES IN THE STUDENT-CENTERED CLASSROOM

Integrating the Techniques into the Classroom

All of these techniques will become a part of your regular classroom routine. You will start with the introduction of TAPPS and Effective Group Process, followed by the Structured Thinking Skills.

The following are some tips to keep students motivated and on task:

- Have something for students to do the minute that they arrive in the classroom.

- Keep the pace and momentum going. Vary the groupings and type of activities that students will do. Use a mixture of individual work, TAPPS pairs, small groups, and whole-class activities.

- Prepare a closing activity in which students reflect on what they have learned.

- Reflect and self-assess on Group Process at different times, sometimes when it is going well, sometimes when it is going badly.

- Set up systems so that students know what they have to do when they finish their work and always have a follow-up activity planned. For example, if they have examined the digestion system using Analyzing the Parts of a Whole, they could then Order by Occurrence the different organs and the role they play in the process of digestion.

Managing Group Process

On occasion, you will find that for one reason or another Group Process breaks down. You never have to give up control if you feel that things are getting out of hand. Have the class stop the activity. Just say that it is time to stop as you do at the end of an Effective Group Process discussion. Then, have students do something calming. They can work individually, use Defining to complete a review activity, write up their notes, or listen to you read aloud. Return to the content that was not completed in a different way during the next lesson. (For more on Effective Group Process, refer to Chapter Four.)

Physical Environment

Here are some tips to think about when setting up your classroom:

CREATE A FLEXIBLE ROOM ARRANGEMENT

- Arrange your room so students are able to move into the appropriate-sized circle as needed. When students are working in small groups and particularly as a whole class, they need to be able to see their classmates' faces.

- Ensure that students can move the furniture easily to suit the work that they are doing.

ESTABLISH SYSTEMS FOR THE STORAGE OF CLASSROOM MATERIALS

- Label storage areas clearly.

- Show students where things can be found and have them return these things to their appropriate places.

- Ensure that basic materials, for example, pens, paper, and so on are easily accessible to students.

Be a Manager of Resources

In a VESC™ lesson, you plan the activities and provide the initial resources. At times, however, students' learning may take them beyond the resources that you provide and they may need to do research using the Internet or the library. Students will often go and look something up when a question arises and bring it back to the next lesson. Alternatively, the teacher can bring back an additional resource to the next lesson.

- You need to organize your resources so they are displayed attractively and are readily available.

- Because students in the class will have different reading abilities, provide material at all reading levels. Students will then be able to choose references they can really use. For example, the life cycle of a frog could be found in a small science picture book or in a high school textbook.

- Have a variety of reference materials available for students, including textbooks, trade books, magazines, newspapers, videos, CD ROMs, and Internet access.

- Where possible, use artifacts, pictures, or posters to introduce or illustrate the curriculum content.

- Ensure that students maintain notebooks where they can put their notes when working through a skill.

- Establish systems for the storage of work. Students may have notebooks and files or folders in which they place completed work.

Use Display to Teach

Use the walls and spaces of your classroom as learning tools. Surround your students with student work and references to guide their work.

- Have the TAPPS and Group Process rules and the steps in the Structured Thinking Skills clearly displayed in the classroom.

- Display the graphic organizers as a reference.

- Display student work that demonstrates use of the skills. Display the whole process, from notes to finished product.

- Take photographs of the students working using the skills and techniques and display them in the classroom.

- Create interactive, works-in-progress that evolve over time such as author studies.

**CLASSROOM MANAGEMENT EXAMPLES
USING VESC™ STRATEGIES**

Establishing Classroom Rules and Procedures

At the beginning of the school year, students can use TAPPS and Group Process to develop the class rules. Students can work in TAPPS pairs to verbalize the type of classroom that they would like to have and then list the rules that they think should exist to make this happen. Then they can use Group Process to share their ideas and create a list of class rules that would help them to work well together.

The skills can also be used to familiarize the students with the physical environment and expectations of the classroom. The following are some examples:

- Examine the different areas of the classroom using Analyzing the Parts of a Whole.

- Play a Categorizing or Grouping game in which they say where they think different objects belong and why.

- Order by Time the routines for beginning the day (and ending the day), for example, hanging up coats, turning in homework, signing-in, coming to the morning meeting circle, and so on.

- Use Categorizing and Grouping to determine the types of activities that they can do when they come into the classroom or when they finish their work, for example, reading, looking through homework or work that the teacher has returned, writing down definitions for any new words that they have learned, Ordering by Occurrence the curriculum content of the lesson, and so on. (The last two are excellent review techniques as well.)

Fine-Tuning Classroom Rules and Procedures

You can also use Effective Group Process to discuss situations in which students are not following rules. For example, if lateness becomes a problem, students might have a Group Process discussion on "being late for class." During the discussion they may talk about the reasons why it important to be on time, the effect of being late on themselves and the rest of the class, reasons for lateness, and ideas for improving punctuality. Prior to a group discussion, you could use a TAPPS exercise as a warm-up activity so that the students have some time to think about the topic they are discussing.

Literacy and the
Ventures Initiative and Focus® System

The limits of your language
are the limits of your world.

—Ludwig Wittgenstein

LITERACY AND THE VENTURES INITIATIVE AND FOCUS® SYSTEM OF STRUCTURED THINKING

15

All of the VESC™ strategies are, at their heart, literacy techniques. Literate people make meaning of what they read, watch, and hear, and can communicate that meaning to others in writing or speech. Practice in the VESC™ strategies is *always* about making meaning and communicating it.

The National Standards focus on the five skills deemed central for developing literacy—reading, writing, speaking, listening, and viewing. In using TAPPS, Effective Group Process, and the Structured Thinking Skills, students are constantly integrating and developing all five of these skills in order to break down, organize, and use information.

Consider, for example, the Constructive Communication technique of Thinking Aloud Paired Problem Solving (TAPPS). One student must figure out and simultaneously explain to a partner what steps to take in order solve a problem while the other student must take notes on these steps and report back to his partner and the class. When engaged in the technique both of these students are honing their ability to communicate at a sophisticated level by integrating reading, writing, listening, and speaking.

The following text lists the second of three Performance Standards In English Language Arts for Speaking, Listening, and Viewing[1] for all grade levels. Each aspect of the standard is addressed in the teaching of Effective Group Process. Students practice and develop each of the behaviors listed below when they are learning and using the technique in the classroom.

E3b The student participates in group meetings, in which the student:

- Displays appropriate turn-taking behaviors

- Actively solicits another person's comment or opinion

- Offers own opinion forcefully without dominating

- Responds appropriately to comments and questions

- Volunteers contributions and responds when directly solicited by teacher or discussion leader

- Gives reasons in support of opinions expressed

- Clarifies, illustrates, or expands on a response when asked to do so; asks classmates for similar expansions

---

[1]Performance Standards, Volumes 1–3 [1997]. National Center on Education and the Economy and the University of Pittsburgh. New Standards, Washington, D.C.

Because *all* VESC™ techniques ask that students verbalize all of their thinking rather than just give one- or two-word answers, students are constantly practicing vocabulary, building logical arguments, defending their points of view, finding support for ideas, making connections, and giving examples. One needs all these skills to communicate successfully in *any* life situation.

Consider the following typical literacy activities students are asked to perform at every grade level and in every subject area. Next to them are the Structured Thinking Skills a student might use to complete each activity successfully.

TYPICAL ACTIVITY OR PROMPT	VESC™ SKILL AND/OR TECHNIQUE
Find the author's main idea in this passage.	Use Supporting a Conclusion to identify the main idea in a passage and its supporting details.
Answer the following questions by reading the accompanying graph.	Use Analyzing the Parts of a Whole to break down the function of each aspect of the graph, and thereby "read" it skillfully to answer each question.
Give your opinion and support it.	Use Supporting a Conclusion to develop both an opinion and its support.
Break down and explain the relationship between each phase in a scientific phenomenon.	Use Ordering by Occurrence to explain the phenomenon step by step and show how each step relates to the ones before and after.
Write an essay in which you explore an important theme in this story and show how the author develops it.	Use Grouping to isolate themes in the story, Ordering by Rank to determine which is most important to write about, and Supporting a Conclusion to show how the author develops it. Students might then employ Ordering by Occurrence to plan their essay.

HOW VESC™ TECHNIQUES SUPPORT EACH OF THE FIVE LITERACY SKILLS

Reading

A class that has practiced TAPPS, Effective Group Process, and at least two of the Structured Thinking Skills is a class equipped with powerful tools for reading. Imagine a classroom in which students have been assigned a difficult passage that they need to work with in order to understand what the author is saying. First, students "TAPPS-through" the reading and share ideas, section by section. Then, the whole class engages in a Group Process discussion in which students contribute their understanding of the piece. Together, they answer the question, "What is important in this text?" Finally, small groups work together to complete a Supporting a Conclusion activity and state an important conclusion about the piece and give support for it. The chalkboards and walls become covered with student ideas and students are ready to write essays—all without the teacher doing any of the thinking for the students.

VESC™ strategies are useful to students in any stage of learning to read. Preliterate students can interact with texts through speaking and listening while their teachers read aloud, ask for reactions, and record what the children have said. Students can also employ VESC™ methods in learning to read. For example, a group of first-grade students can decode and learn high-frequency words such as "cat," "the," "went," and "play" by using verbalization techniques to build knowledge of letter–sound relationships. Similarly, high school biology students can wrestle with "meiosis," "chromosome," "gamete," and "zygote" through a Defining and Describing exercise in which they become familiar with their meanings, followed by problem solving using these terms in TAPPS pairs, concluding in a Grouping and Categorizing exercise.

Because our goal is to give students tools they can use to learn more efficiently and skillfully for the rest of their lives, we treat reading as thinking. Students are shown how to use the tools they have—TAPPS, Group Process, and the Structured Thinking Skills— to structure and make meaning of what they read. A teacher might assign a chapter on World War II and ask students to complete a Grouping and Categorizing exercise in which they compile information on the roles of different countries in the conflict. When they have finished reading, the students could draw some conclusions about these different roles.

As students understand and internalize these skills, they are able to choose one or more skills to break down complex material. When they find themselves facing difficult reading in a situation like a standardized test, they have tools that help them facilitate their own understanding.

Writing

We often ask students to write essays or turn in reports in which they are to summarize, analyze, or apply information. As in the preceding examples with reading, when you bring more structure to bear on these assignments, students will be much more skilled at doing the job.

VESC™ teachers help students break down writing tasks by deciding which skill or series of skills best fit the purpose of the writing assignment. In the last step of each Structured Thinking Skill, students write a summary statement or interpretation about the information they have just organized. Having systematically broken down information into a useable form, students are prepared to elaborate on a conclusion in their writing. For example, if students in a social studies class are asked to write an essay comparing and contrasting two forms of government, the summary statement or interpretation that they derive after doing an Examining Similarities and Differences activity easily becomes their thesis statement. The significance of similarities and differences they have identified support this conclusion.

The chart below demonstrates how each of the Structured Thinking Skills can be used as a starting point for accomplishing the different types of writing required by the state and national standards.

STRUCTURED THINKING SKILL	TYPE OF WRITING
Defining	To create short explanatory paragraphs
Describing	Descriptive writing to create a mental image, an explanation, or provide insight, humor, or inspiration
Examining Similarities and Differences	Compare and Contrast essay
Analyzing the Parts of a Whole	Descriptive essay
Grouping and Categorizing	Descriptive essay
Ordering	Narrative essay or procedure
Supporting a Conclusion	Persuasive essay

In a VESC™ classroom, writing covers the walls. This writing is constantly changing and being updated. In many classrooms, only "finished products" are seen as fit to be on the walls. In a VESC™ classroom, finished products are displayed, but writing is more frequently a record or graphic organization of ongoing thinking. Students continue to use this information, refer to it, and interact with it. They read what they have written to themselves and/or an audience to check for understanding. As they take on more responsibility for their own learning, students write more skillfully and independently. Writing becomes a means to an end—a tool for thinking.

Speaking and Listening

In many classrooms, students rarely speak or do so in an artificial way. In general, the teacher does most of the talking; students talk only when called on to give a one- or two-word answer to a teacher's question. Most "classroom talk" does not resemble the engaged, active way students speak when they are not in class.

In a VESC™ classroom, by contrast, speaking and listening occur constantly and naturally. Students speak and listen to ask real questions, to make meaning of things together, and to get information they need. There is a natural give-and-take, whether in pairs, small groups, or with the class as a whole. A good Group Process discussion involving the whole class resembles a real conversation.

Learning is a social process. If you cannot communicate your understanding to another person, you have not truly learned it. TAPPS teaches students to slow down their thinking and make it clear to others, in part as a check on the thinking itself. If you are working through a problem silently to yourself, you can easily skip steps and not solve the problem correctly or completely. If you must make your process plain to another person, however, you are less likely to skip steps. Similarly, if you must listen carefully to understand another person's thinking process, you cannot listen in the passive way students in more traditional classes often listen to each other. The answer students work toward is for themselves, not the teacher.

As students work with the VESC™ strategies they are developing lifelong tools for literacy.

LITERACY AND STRUCTURED THINKING

Knowledge of the methods and structured thinking strategies introduced in this book can really help your students on their journey to becoming highly literate independent learners. The strategies that you have learned so far integrate mental processing and content. They make the nature of the mental processing explicit to the students. Using this approach in your classroom will help students develop their comprehension and expression abilities. Students can successfully incorporate structured thinking into speaking, listening, viewing, reading, and writing.

Some Methods for Developing Comprehension and Expression

The final section in the book deals with some methods that deal with Comprehension and Expression and can be easily implemented into the classroom.
These are:

- Literature Circles

- Author Study

- Using Grouping or Categorization frameworks to study multiple texts.

Literature Circles

Many English Language Arts teachers currently use some version of Literature Circles but they can be used with students in all subjects. More structured than simple small-group discussions, literature circles are small groups in which students discuss a text they have all read. This text might be a novel or story, but could just as easily be a biography of a scientist, historical text, or newspaper article on a current event or discovery. Because discussion is focused on what students read with a small group of peers rather than the class as a whole, Literature Circles are less intimidating than traditional all-class discussions. They can play a large role in encouraging students to read and to talk to their peers regularly and naturally about what they read.

In some forms of literature circles, structure is created by assigning roles. In the VESC™ classroom, this is not necessary. In fact, in the VESC™ classroom literature circles should feel quite natural and easy to implement—after all, your students have been practicing the Rules of Effective Group Process Discussion. Think of Literature Circles as mini Group Process discussions.

HOW TO IMPLEMENT LITERATURE CIRCLES IN YOUR CLASSROOM

1. The teacher or students choose a relatively high-interest text. It is important for students to be able to choose their own texts some of the time.

2. The class reviews the rules of Effective Group Process.

 POINTER:

The first few times students try Literature Circles, you may need to discuss the rules and expectations as a whole class first. For example, you might ask students, "Which of the rules of Group Process might be harder to follow in Literature Circles than when you are in whole-class Group Discussions?" "Which might be easier?" "Why?"

3. The teacher divides students into small groups of between five and seven students. You can create these groupings based on any criteria you feels are important (mixed reading level, similar books for those classes where individuals or groups have been reading different texts, similar skill level, etc.). Group composition might remain constant throughout the year, or might change at fixed points like a change of semester or unit. Some teachers allow students to choose their own group composition.

4. Work with students to create a process to choose a facilitator for each group. This facilitator is responsible for doing what the facilitator in all Group Process Discussions does—reading the piece (or a section of it) aloud, asking students for questions, choosing a question to start, and keeping time during the discussion. At the end of the discussion, the facilitator should ask the participants to assess their behavior against the Rules of Group Process.

5. To start, groups might be given ten or so minutes for discussion. The teacher can walk around the room and observe, but should refrain from entering into any of the discussions. At the end of ten minutes, facilitators of the individual groups should ask participants to stop and assess themselves against the Rules of Group Process.

6. Finally the whole class should come together discuss how the process went, what help or adaptations they might need, what problems developed, or other issues they want to raise. Students might also be asked to keep individual journals or other written records of their Literature Circle discussions.

 POINTER:

You may want to do a "fishbowl" when first practicing Literature Circles, or whenever intervention is needed. In this technique, you ask for a group to volunteer to be observed by the rest of the class as they conduct their discussion. Group members sit in the middle of the room while the rest of the class sits in a circle around them (the "fishbowl") and takes notes on their discussion. Afterwards, the small group members assess themselves against the rules of Group Process. The larger group then takes a turn making constructive comments on their process.

AUTHOR STUDY

An author study can be used so help students gain in depth knowledge of the works by a given author. Author studies help students become familiar with a number of authors. They allow them to become familiar with the writing style of an author and to make comparisons between authors. The activities that are part of an author study will help the students meet the state standards for literacy.

Using an author study in the classroom results in students:

- Being able to discuss authors and their work.
- Taking part in discussions that have a literature focus.
- Building a community that has some shared literature experience.
- Developing their literacy skills.
- Creating meaning from text.
- Using the skills good readers use.
- Developing a common core of information.
- Making connections between text to self, text to text, and text to others.
- Accessing information they need but might not be able to because of their reading abilities.

What is Involved in an Author Study?

SELECTING AUTHORS

The first thing a teacher must do is select an author or a series of authors to be studied during the year.

INTRODUCING THE AUTHOR TO THE STUDENTS

The following are some suggestions:

- Display book covers and encourage children to speculate as to the content.
- Read aloud sample passages from a number of books and ask children what they think the rest of the story might be about.
- Show a video about the author. Provide a focus for each segment of the video you show.
- Read about an author.
- Save work from previous classes to display prior to introducing an author.
- Find Web sites about the author.

READING THE BOOKS

- If children cannot read the books, you can read them aloud.
- If children can read the books, read aloud one of the author's books and make available all or most of the other books the author has written. Children can then form Literature Circles for discussion purposes.

WORKING WITH THE BOOKS

The purpose here is have the children be able to identify the works of an author and also be able to talk about the body of an author's work. There are many ways to accomplish this.

EXTENDING INTEREST IN AN AUTHOR AND HIS OR HER BOOKS

You can use Structured Thinking Skills to extend students' interest in an author and his or her books. For example, Examining Similarities and Differences is an effective way of encouraging children to discuss an author or to compare two authors. Working with the art specialist is also another way of enriching students' experience with an author's work.

Example 10-day Author Study Using Picture Books

PLANNING STAGE

- Select the author and gather the books.

- Gather the index cards, markers, and crayons.

- Create a categorization grid to use for Day 1 through Day 5 on large chart paper. See the sample blank grid below. A sample author study grid, based on the work of Tomie dePaola, follows this section.

	DAY 1	DAY 2	DAY 3	DAY 4	DAY 5
Characters					
Setting					
Problem					
Solutions					
Interesting Language					

IMPLEMENTING STAGE

Day One: Reading the First Text
- Students sit in a circle as in an Effective Group Process Discussion. Read the text aloud to them.

- Follow this with a Group Process discussion. You may ask students to focus on a particular element of the story, e.g., characters and character traits. If the idea of story elements is new for the students you could introduce them using Analyzing the Parts of a Whole.

- Record on the chart all the story elements for the first text.

Day Two: Introducing the Second Text

- Students sit in a circle as in an Effective Group Process Discussion. Ask them to talk about yesterday's story. Once again, you may ask them to focus on a particular aspect. Read the second text aloud to the students.

- Follow this with a Group Process Discussion. You may ask students to focus on a particular element of the story, e.g., settings within the story.

- Record on the chart all the story elements for the second text.

Day Three: Introducing the Third Text

- Students sit in a circle as in an Effective Group Process Discussion. Ask them to talk about yesterday's story. Once again, you may ask them to focus on a particular aspect. Read the third text aloud to the students.

- Follow this with a Group Process Discussion. You may ask students to focus on a particular element of the story, e.g., the conflict or problem in the story.

  Record on the chart all the story elements for the third text.

Day Four: Introducing the Fourth Text

- Students sit in a circle as in an Effective Group Process Discussion. Ask them to talk about yesterday's story. Once again, you may ask them to focus on a particular aspect. Read the fourth text aloud to the students.

- Follow this with a Group Process Discussion. You may ask students to focus on a particular element of the story, e.g., solution of the story.

- Record on the chart all the story elements for the fourth text.

Day Five: Introducing the Fifth Text

- Students sit in a circle as in an Effective Group Process Discussion. Ask them to talk about yesterday's story. Once again, you may ask them to focus on a particular aspect. Read the fifth text aloud to the students.

- Follow this with a Group Process Discussion. You may ask students to focus on a particular element of the story, e.g., interesting language in the story.

- Record on the chart all the story elements for the fifth text.

Students are now familiar with five works by a particular author. During the second week, students can revisit the texts using different Structured Thinking Skills:

- Ordering by Occurrence the events in one or more of the stories.

- Ordering by Rank the characters in one or more of the stories.

- Using Analyzing the Parts of a Whole to examine the different elements of one or more of the stories.

- Examining Similarities and Differences between two of the texts, two characters in a story or different stories, or a character at the beginning and end of a story.

- Using Analyzing the Parts of a Whole to examine the different characters in a particular story.

- Categorizing or Grouping the different settings in a story.

- Categorizing different vocabulary in a text, (e.g., words beginning with st-, ch-, or sl-).

- Find the longest or shortest words (adjectives, verbs, common nouns) in the text.

- Use Categorizing and Supporting a Conclusion to examine any themes that run through the author's work.

- Examining Similarities and Differences between this author's work with the work of another author.

IDEAS FOR EXTENSION ACTIVITIES

- Student publication of their own versions or adaptations of the stories

- Artwork—painting, printing, or collage mobiles—based on the books

- Puppet shows or plays based on the books

- Student production of story tapes to accompany the books

- Developing word walls based on the author study

The VESC™ approach to literacy is a balanced approach. Though we believe in the efficacy of constructivist methods, we do not prescribe any particular program for the teaching of literacy. Instead, we urge teachers to approach literacy as we urge you to approach any kind of thinking: with structure. We approach reading, writing, listening, speaking, and viewing by being conscious and deliberate about the thinking inherent in any activity we ask students to do.

SAMPLE AUTHOR STUDY: TOMIE DEPAOLA

TITLE	CHARACTERS	SETTING	PROBLEM	SOLUTION	INTERESTING WORDS
Pancakes for Breakfast	Woman Neighbors Assorted pets	House, farm	Woman wants pancakes and encounters obstacles in making them.	She goes to the neighbors' house for pancakes.	No words
The Popcorn Book	Two brothers	Their house	The boys want to know why their mom keeps popcorn in the refrigerator.	They read a book and find out that popcorn is best stored in the refrigerator so it stays moist.	"old maids" Algonquians Iroquois San Salvador Columbus
Nana Upstairs and Nana Downstairs	Tommy His grand-mother His great-grandmother	Grand-mother's house His house	Tommy is very close to his 94-year-old great-grandmother, but she dies. Eventually his grandmother dies, too.	Tommy comes to terms with these deaths by imagining that shooting (falling) stars are kisses form his nanas, now both "upstairs."	Falling star Silver-white hair Cow's tail
The Legend of Old Befana	Old Befana Three Kings Little boy	Small town	An old woman encounters three kings, who say they are on their way to visit a Child King. They are bringing gifts. The Old Befana decides that she, too, will search for the Baby King and bring gifts.	She "flies" on her broom but she cannot find the child. Instead, she visits other children and leaves gifts for them.	Befana splendid procession Bethlehem Miracles Alas
Strega Nona	Strega Nona Anthony	A town in Calabria, Italy	Strega Nona has a magic pasta pot. Anthony borrows the pot, says magic words, and the pot makes more pasta then the whole town can eat.	Strega Nona comes home just in time to say some magic words and stop the pasta before it overtakes the town. As his punishment, Anthony must eat the pasta.	Pasta Calabria grazie sputter

USING A CLASSIFICATION OR CATEGORIZATION FRAMEWORK ACROSS CONTENT AREAS TO STUDY MULTIPLE TEXTS

The framework used as part of the author study can be adapted to fit any subject area and any kind of material. The structure it uses simply provides a way to look at elements that multiple texts have in common in dealing with one subject, author, or genre. For example, a class in each of the following subject areas might use this Grouping or Classification Framework to do the following:

English Language Arts

- Author studies

- Genre studies (e.g., the personal essay, the coming-of-age story, myths, poetry, the mystery and detective novel, the short story, sports writing, humor writing, etc.)

- Character studies (the hero, the villain, women in literature, etc.)

- Advertising studies (the approaches used to entice buyers in different kinds of advertising, etc.)

- Literary Era studies (looking at multiple texts from the Victorian Era, the Renaissance, the 1920's, etc.)

- Geographical Studies (the literature of New England, the American West, Australia, etc.)

Social Studies

- Genre studies (speeches, oral histories, political cartoons, campaign materials, treaties, etc.)

- Map studies (maps as they change over time, different kinds of maps, ways of using maps, etc.)

- Area studies (multiple texts as they describe and analyze the same city, country, or region)

- Historical figure studies (multiple texts, including biography, autobiography, political cartoons, editorials, or any other kind of analysis as they describe and analyze historical figures)

- Current event studies (looking at how different media treat the same current event, using political cartoons, television news, newspaper and magazine reporting, editorials, etc.)

SAMPLE CLASSIFICATION FRAMEWORK AND ACTIVITIES FOR A HIGH SCHOOL ENGLISH CLASS GENRE STUDY OF "THE COMING-OF-AGE STORY"

Below are examples of coming-of-age works and of the aspects of the genre that you might have students examine. For example, most coming-of-age stories feature significant portions that deal with the main character's relationship with his or her family. Teachers might use the categories listed below, or create, with their students, their own classifications of those aspects common to the coming-of-age story.

TITLE OF WORK	OPENING SCENES	VOICE/POINT OF VIEW	RELATIONSHIP WITH FAMILY	TURNING POINT(S)	FRIENDSHIP(S)
Catcher in the Rye					
Kaffir Boy					
Stand By Me					
The House on Mango Street					
A Tree Grows in Brooklyn					

Sample exercises using the completed grid:

- Examine your grid and highlight the areas in which you find particularly strong similarities among the different works. What conclusions can you draw from these similarities?

- Use Analyzing the Parts of a Whole to examine the typical parts of the coming-of-age story. Then take each work and identify each of the parts that appear in it.

- Taking each category cited above, Order by Rank which work did the best job of portraying that aspect of the coming-of-age story. For example, which portrayed relationship with family in the most interesting or most complex way? Compare your answers with those of your classmates. What conclusions can you draw overall about what makes for excellence in a film or literary depiction of "coming of age"?

- Draw a conclusion about the coming-of-age story in general, and support it with as many specific reasons and examples from these works as possible. Use this as a basis for an essay that sums up something important you have learned about this genre.

- Find lines or scenes from each work that echo lines or scenes in one or more of the other works. Put them together in some way (e.g., as a dialogue, play, or poem) and read them aloud to your classmates.

- Now that you have read and watched several stories from the same genre, what would you list as some of the clichés of the coming-of-age story? Look for those characters, realizations, turning points, and themes that seem to appear repeatedly and seem particularly difficult to make "fresh" each time. Use Grouping and include examples.

- Which main character from one coming-of-age story would have the best advice to give the main character from another story? Perhaps both characters go through the same experience, one more successfully than the other, or perhaps one finds a better way of dealing with a troublesome relationship or issue. Staying true to the character's voice, write the advice this character would give the other, stating at what point in the advisee's story the advice would best be given.

SAMPLE CLASSIFICATION FRAMEWORK AND ACTIVITIES FOR AN EARTH SCIENCE TOPIC STUDY OF VOLCANOES

You can use a similar framework to help students reflect on how they use information on a particular topic. This example deals with volcanoes. Provide each group of students with a selection of resources on the topic. These may include books, Internet sites, posters, or actual artifacts. Students then complete a classification grid similar to the one below. The categories can vary depending on what they are studying and the nature of the texts. Students can create similar frameworks independently when working on individual projects.

TITLE AND AUTHOR	TYPE OF TEXT	INFORMATION IN THE TEXT	USING STRUCTURED THINKING SKILLS TO PROCESS THE INFORMATION	INTERESTING VOCABULARY
Violent Volcanoes, by Anita Garner	From *Horrible Geography* series. Text, diagrams and cartoons about volcanoes. Divided into chapters.	Types of volcano Parts of a volcano Volcanic eruptions Effects of a volcanic eruption Extinct and active volcanoes	Grouping and Categorizing Analyzing the Parts of a Whole Ordering by Occurrence Examining Cause and Effect Examining Similarities and Differences	cone, crater, pipe, active, dormant, lava, lapilli, vesuvius, jungle bath
Volcanoes and Earthquakes, by Dr. Eldridge Moores (Consulting Editor)	Color book containing text, photos and diagrams. Has glossary and index.	Types of volcanic eruptions Parts of a volcano Types of lava flow Famous volcanoes	Grouping and Categorizing Analyzing the Parts of a Whole Grouping and Categorizing Ordering by Time different eruptions	sill, pillow lava, pyroclastic flow, year without summer, mudflow, avalanches
Volcanoes, by Seymour Simon	Fairly simple text and great photographs volcanoes.	Types of volcanoes Effects of volcanic eruptions Strato and composite volcanoes	Grouping and Categorizing Examining Cause and Effect Examining Similarities and Differences	magma, fiery rivers, ten million tons of dynamite, badly damaged, giant cracked eggshells.
Encyclopedia of our Awesome Earth, by Liz White (Editor)	One chapter on volcanoes with text and color illustrations.	Parts of a volcano Active, dormant, and extinct volcanoes Volcanologist's equipment	Analyzing the Parts of a Whole Defining and Describing Analyzing the Parts of a Whole	volcanologist, lava bombs, bubbling minerals, black smokers, blanket of black ash, *pahoehoe*
Hawaiian Volcano Observatory, USGS	http://wwwhvo.wr.usgs.gov/kilauea/ Photographs, text, current data on eruptions.	The world's most active volcano	Describing Ordering by Time recent volcanic activity.	volcano goddess, spewing, much spreading, caldera

CONCLUSION

All Students Can Learn

CONCLUSION: ALL STUDENTS CAN LEARN

The strategies that you have read about in *Constructive Communication and Structured Thinking in the Classroom, Volume 1* will help you create a classroom in which students are active participants in their learning. As you and your students become more adept with each of the strategies you will see their versatility. The way that you combine strategies and methods or use them in sequence makes them powerful learning tools.

TEACHER OUTCOMES

An awareness of the ideas behind and implementation of the strategies will develop your skill and professionalism as an educator in many ways including the following:

- The creation of a classroom environment where the student-centered learning is paramount. You will strive to be a facilitator or coach of students' learning, ensuring that the students have the maximum opportunity to engage with and process the curriculum content, keeping the amount of teacher talk time to the minimum.

- The use of learning strategies that result in students being able to problem solve, apply, and retain what they have learned.

- Developing an awareness of factors that affect mental processing and how teacher behavior can impede the students' development as independent learners and making modifications accordingly. Becoming skilled at intervening in ways that do not shut down students' thinking.

- Planning strategically in a way that focuses on student outcomes. Using assessment to inform planning and differentiating curriculum and activities so that the different learning needs of students are met and maximum potential is realized.

- As the techniques become routine you will find that they help minimize behavior and discipline problems.

- Pacing lessons to maintain student interest.

- Not expecting students to do what they have not been taught. There is explicit teaching of all the mental processes that the student is required to engage in.

- Being a reference for students. Providing them with the information that they want to know. Providing resources that will help them find the answers to their questions.

Students can use these tools when working alone, with a partner, in a small group, or as part of a whole class. It is important to remember that these strategies and methods are vehicles or tools for learning. Students should have the opportunity to use them in ways that best serve their needs as learners.

STUDENT OUTCOMES

The Structured Thinking Strategies in *Constructive Communication and Structured Thinking in the Classroom, Volume 1* equip learners with the skills to manage and communicate their thinking and learning in many ways including the following:

- A developed awareness of what causes shutdown in themselves and others and the strategies to stay or get back on task.

- The ability to share their ideas and listen to the ideas of others. They help develop a real understanding of the benefits of working in a group.

- The ability to be frank about their learning, to admit when they do not know something and seek clarification when something is not clear.

- A knowledge of strategies that can be used to tackle challenging texts and structure writing to improve literacy standards.

- A series of strategies and methods that students use to learn *any* information. This includes both academic and everyday knowledge.

- A variety of ways to represent their thinking including organizing information graphically, structuring written information, and creating charts and diagrams.

- The ability to think critically, skillfully and systematically and also monitor thinking for accuracy.

- The ability to be tenacious self-driven learners who are neither thwarted by an academically rigorous curriculum nor dependent solely on teacher praise or other extrinsic goals.

In short, the students now have a variety of tools that will allow them to begin the journey to becoming independent, academically successful lifelong learners.

TAKING IT TO THE NEXT LEVEL

As you work with these strategies you will find that they become part of your classroom routine and you and your students will use them with ease. In *Constructive Communication and Structured Thinking in the Classroom, Volume 2*, you will learn more advanced structured thinking strategies and become more proficient in the creation of lessons that systematically build the students' abilities to develop what commonly is called higher order thinking.

Over time and with practice students will develop the ability to recognize the type of thinking and mental steps necessary to respond to both simple and more complex assignments. The successful completion of such assignments, in a way that exceeds the requirements of state standards will often require the use of a variety of skills and strategies. You will find a more in depth development of this idea in the *Constructive Communication and Structured Thinking in the Classroom, Volume 2*. The teacher and student work together to develop mental strategies that will help the student build meaning and understanding of curriculum content.

APPENDIX A

Constructive Communication
Resources

THE VENTURES INITIATIVE AND FOCUS®
SYSTEM OF STRUCTURED THINKING

STRUCTURED THINKING STRATEGIES

COMPREHENSION STRATEGIES
Purpose: To understand the significant characteristics of key concepts and to draw interpretations or inferences about them.
- Structured Concept Learning
- Describing and Defining
- Literacy
- Mathematical Thinking
- Informational Literacy
- Academic Preparedness Skills

$\updownarrow$

ANALYTIC THINKING STRATEGIES
Purpose: To understand how significant concepts or processes are interrelated.
- Examining Similarities and Differences
- Analyzing the Parts of a Whole
- Categorizing and Grouping
- Ordering
  - by Time
  - by Occurrence
  - by Rank
- Supporting a Conclusion
  - Examining My Own Conclusion
  - Examining an Author's Conclusion

$\updownarrow$

EVALUATIVE THINKING STRATEGIES
Purpose: To evaluate conclusions or actions based on principles of sound reasoning and reliable information.
- Evaluating Causes
- Evaluating Predictions
- Evaluating Sources of Information
- Evaluating Decisions
- Evaluating Conclusions
  - Conditional Statements
  - Reasons and Assumptions

$\updownarrow$

PRODUCTIVE THINKING STRATEGIES
Purpose: To create original expressions of learned material.
- Generating Ideas
- Creating Analogies and Metaphors
- The Decision-Making Process
  - Decision Framing
  - Analyzing Alternatives
  - Evaluating Alternatives
- Composition Skills
- Problem-Based Learning (PBL)

METHODS

$\leftrightarrow$ **CONSTRUCTIVE COMMUNICATION**
- Thinking Aloud Paired Problem Solving
- Visualization
- Effective Group Process
- Assessing Prior Knowledge

$\leftrightarrow$ **STRUCTURED THINKING SKILLS AND PROCESSES**
- Making thinking explicit
- Graphic organization of information
- Metacognitive questioning
- Identifying the relation of Structured Thinking Skills to Problem-Based Learning (PBL) and Structured Project Learning (SPL)

$\leftrightarrow$ **COMPREHENSION AND EXPRESSION**
- Visualization (rebuilding models)
- Literature Circles
- Author Study
- Comprehension and expression of Structured Thinking
- Structured Project Learning (SPL)

$\Downarrow$

ACADEMIC ACHIEVEMENT AND EFFECTIVE LIFELONG LEARNING

THINKING ALOUD PAIRED PROBLEM SOLVING
(TAPPS)

PROBLEM SOLVER	LISTENER
Begin by reading the problem aloud to the Listener.	Remind the Problem Solver to continue verbalizing his or her thinking if the Problem Solver stops talking.
Say every thought that goes through your mind as you attempt to solve the problem.	Question the Problem Solver only if the Problem Solver does not fully explain a step being taken in solving the problem.
Never stop talking to the Listener.	Do not offer help in solving the problem or correct an answer.
Use paper and pencil if you need to, but do not stop talking.	You can take notes on what the Problem Solver is saying and doing. When everyone is finished, you may be asked to explain what the Problem Solver did.

THINKING ALOUD PAIRED PROBLEM SOLVING
(TAPPS)

PROBLEM SOLVER	LISTENER
Begin by reading the problem aloud to the Listener.	Remind the Problem Solver to continue verbalizing his or her thinking if the Problem Solver stops talking.
Say every thought that goes through your mind as you attempt to solve the problem.	Question the Problem Solver only if the Problem Solver does not fully explain a step being taken in solving the problem.
Verbalize each step you take and the reason for doing so; do not expect the Listener to understand without your doing so.	Do not offer help in solving the problem or correct an answer.
Never stop talking to the Listener.	Do not indicate whether you agree or disagree with the Problem Solver.
Use paper and pencil if you need to, but do not stop talking.	Keep the process going!
Respond to the Listener's questions when the Listener does not understand what you said.	Take notes on what the Problem Solver is saying and doing. When everyone is finished, you may be asked to explain what the Problem Solver did and why it was done.

TAPPS SELF-ASSESSMENT

Today's Date:						
My Role (Problem Solver or Listener):						
My Partner's Name:						
PROBLEM SOLVER	**LISTENER**	**MY BEHAVIOR (+ OR -)**				
Begin by reading the problem aloud to the Listener.	Remind the Problem Solver to continue verbalizing his or her thinking if the Problem Solver stops talking.					
Say every thought that goes through your mind as you attempt to solve the problem.	Question the Problem Solver only if the Problem Solver does not fully explain a step being taken in solving the problem.					
Never stop talking to the Listener.	Do not offer help in solving the problem or correct an answer.					
Use paper and pencil if you need to, but do not stop talking.	You can take notes on what the Problem Solver is saying and doing. When everyone is finished, you may be asked to explain what the Problem Solver did.					

TAPPS SELF-ASSESSMENT

Today's Date					
My Role (Problem Solver or Listener)					
My Partner's Name					
PROBLEM SOLVER	**LISTENER**	**MY BEHAVIOR (+ OR -)**			
Begin by reading the problem aloud to the Listener.	Remind the Problem Solver to continue verbalizing his or her thinking if the Problem Solver stops talking.				
Say every thought that goes through your mind as you attempt to solve the problem.	Question the Problem Solver only if the Problem Solver does not fully explain a step being taken in solving the problem.				
Verbalize each step you take and the reason for doing so; do not expect the Listener to understand without your doing so.	Do not offer help in solving the problem or correct an answer.				
Never stop talking to the Listener.	Do not indicate whether you agree or disagree with the Problem Solver.				
Use paper and pencil if you need to, but do not stop talking.	Keep the process going!				
Respond to the Listener's questions when the Listener does not understand what you said.	Take notes on what the Problem Solver is saying and doing. When everyone is finished, you may be asked to explain what the Problem Solver did and why it was done.				

PROBLEM SOLVER

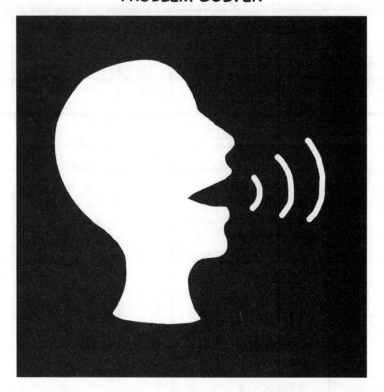

LISTENER

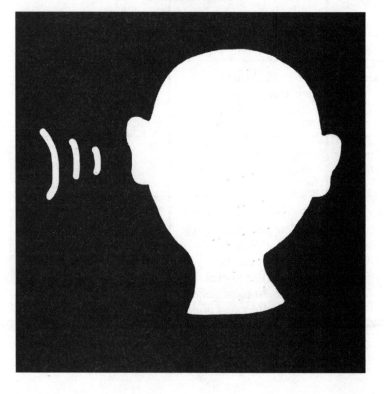

EFFECTIVE GROUP PROCESS RULES

1. Sit in a circle so you can see everyone.

2. Listen to the teacher read aloud while you follow along.

3. Do not speak when others are talking.

4. Listen and respond to what your classmates are saying in a respectful way.

5. Do not have side conversations.

6. Join in the discussion.

EFFECTIVE GROUP PROCESS RULES

1. Sit in a circle so you can see everyone.

2. Stay focused on the material.

3. Maintain order by controlling the impulse to speak when others are speaking.

4. Maintain a respectful attitude towards different perspectives.

5. Listen carefully as the discussion proceeds.

6. Respond clearly to comments and questions.

7. Seek clarification in a way that keeps the communication constructive.

8. Refrain from having side conversations

9. You have a responsibility to participate.

A QUICK GUIDE TO STUDENT BEHAVIOR USING EFFECTIVE GROUP PROCESS DISCUSSION

BEFORE THE DISCUSSION, STUDENTS

- Arrange themselves in the appropriate seating arrangement quickly and quietly

- Actively listen to and/or view the material carefully

- Formulate a question for discussion based on the material

- Read their question loudly and clearly

DURING THE DISCUSSION, STUDENTS

- Maintain order in the group by controlling the impulse to speak while others are speaking

- Remember the comments of others in the group as the discussion proceeds

- Maintain a respectful attitude toward different perspectives

- Respond clearly to comments and questions

- Seek clarification in a way that keeps the communication constructive

- Refrain from side conversations

- Keep thinking and working with the group even through rough patches in the discussion

AFTER THE DISCUSSION, STUDENTS

- Honestly assess the discussion in terms of how the group followed the rules of Effective Group Process Discussion

EFFECTIVE GROUP PROCESS
SELF-ASSESSMENT

EFFECTIVE GROUP PROCESS RULES	MY BEHAVIOR
1. Sit in a circle so you can see everyone.	
2. Listen to the teacher read aloud while you follow along.	
3. Do not speak when others are talking.	
4. Listen and respond to what your classmates are saying in a respectful way.	
5. Do not have side conversations.	
6. Join in the discussion.	
Conclusion regarding my behavior toward achieving Effective Group Process:	

EFFECTIVE GROUP PROCESS
SELF-ASSESSMENT

EFFECTIVE GROUP PROCESS RULES	MY BEHAVIOR
1. Sit in a circle so you can see everyone.	
2. Stay focused on the material.	
3. Maintain order by controlling the impulse to speak when others are speaking.	
4. Maintain a respectful attitude towards different perspectives.	
5. Listen carefully as the discussion proceeds.	
6. Respond clearly to comments and questions.	
7. Seek clarification in a way that keeps the communication constructive.	
8. Refrain from having side conversations	
9. You have a responsibility to participate.	
Conclusion regarding my behavior toward achieving Effective Group Process:	

EFFECTIVE GROUP PROCESS
SELF-REFLECTION

1. Did you sometimes want to speak while someone else was talking?	
2. Did you speak to your neighbor instead of the group?	
3. Did you sometimes want to interrupt another speaker's comments when that speaker was obviously wrong?	
4. Did you mentally remove yourself from the discussion when the discussion focused on error?	
5. Did you find it difficult to interact with other individuals you believed to be less competent than you consider yourself to be?	
6. Did you want to tell a particular individual to stop dominating the conversation?	
7. Did you want to ask an individual why he or she refused to enter the discussion?	
8. Did you ever mentally abandon the discussion because you were unable to inject your comments?	
9. Did you ever have difficulty understanding another individual's comments?	
10. Did you ever have difficulty understanding the relationship of one person's comments to the discussion topic?	
11. Did you ever experience a "lost" feeling during the discussion?	
12. Did you have difficulty stating your perspective without becoming confrontational or belligerent?	
13. Did you ever ask yourself how could one stay in the discussion yet maintain the guidelines?	
14. Did you ever ask yourself if this was worth all the trouble?	
15. Did you lose interest if you were not doing the talking and you did not agree with the speaker?	

APPENDIX B

Structured Thinking Skills Resources

TEACHER SELF-REFLECTION:
INTRODUCING A STRUCTURED THINKING SKILL

Did I tell students the name of the skill I am going to teach?	
Did I offer a simple explanation of the skill by showing how one uses it in everyday life?	
Did I choose simple material with which to demonstrate the skill the first time so that students can concentrate on the steps without the distraction of difficult material?	
Did I state the steps of the skill clearly?	
Did I explain to the class beforehand that I would not be commenting on or questioning their thinking, but simply writing down what they say? Did I explain that it is the responsibility of their fellow students to question each other's contributions if they are not satisfied with them?	
Did I remind the class of the importance of Effective Group Process in being able to evaluate others' responses?	
Did I facilitate the skill by writing down EXACTLY what they said for each step, without questioning or changing their words?	
Did I refrain from offering "feedback" on their responses, such as saying "good!" to some responses?	
Did I use structures for encouraging them to talk taking into account their ability to communicate with each other? (For example, if my class does not have the Group Process skills to consider constructively and systematically every step of the skill as a large group, did I break them into pairs or small groups, or let them work alone for some of the steps?)	
Did each student individually take written notes for every step of the skill, recording his or her own thinking and/or class comments?	
Did I ask each student individually to write an interpretation or summary statement of some kind?	
Did I remember throughout the process not to do students' thinking for them, but only to act as a resource for their questions?	

TEACHER SELF-REFLECTION:
USING A STRUCTURED THINKING SKILL

Did I tell my students which skill we would be using and remind them of the steps of that skill?	
Did I give them more difficult material this time than I did the first time?	
Did I again remind them to follow the rules of Group Process in discussing their thinking?	
Did I facilitate the steps of the skill without thinking for them, offering comment or praise, or changing their words when I recorded their comments?	
Did I observe any growth in my students' abilities to use this technique and/or communicate their thinking with each other?	

How?

Next time I use this skill, how may I facilitate it to encourage further growth in my students' ability to use it and to communicate with each other?

STUDENT SELF-REFLECTION:
USING A STRUCTURED THINKING SKILL

Do I know what Structured Thinking Skill I am using?	
Can I state how and why I am using this skill right now? (For example, you might say, "I am using the skill of Examining Similarities and Differences to learn about the processes of meiosis and mitosis.").	
Can I state the steps in the skill?	
As I applied each of the steps to the content or information, can I state which step I was using?	
Did I reach a conclusion that allows me to use the original information—to complete a task, answer a question, or write a paper?	
What happened as I went through the mental steps of this skill in applying it to this content?	
Were any steps in the skill particularly difficult? Why?	

245

DEFINING

Step One: Name the large group to which the item belongs.

Step Two: Give enough attributes to set the item apart from every other member of the group. Ask, "Have I identified enough attributes to set it apart?" "Do other members share these attributes?" If they do, state more.

Step Three: Now state a definition, for example, "A _____ is_____."

DEFINING

Step One: Name the large category to which the item belongs.

Step Two: State enough defining attributes to set the item apart from every other member of the category.

Use this question as a check: "Have I identified enough attributes to set it apart from all other members of the group?" If not, state more attributes.

Step Three: State a definition.

DESCRIBING

Step One: Close your eyes and try to see the thing that you are describing.

Step Two: Think about the different aspects of the thing that you are going to describe: size, shape, color, texture, smell, sound, etc.

Step Three: Use each of the aspects to describe the object.

Step Four: Read your description to your classmates. Do they know what you are describing?

DESCRIBING

Step One: State the purpose of the description, i.e., humor, explanation, insight, inspiration, or esthetic.

Step Two: Create a mental picture of the item.

Step Three: Verbalize the attributes of each item: size, shape, color, texture, smell, sound, etc.

Step Four: Verbalize how each attribute is significant, using analogies or making connections with prior knowledge.

Step Five: Add details by developing words and phrases that accurately communicate your mental picture to others.

Step Six: Restate or read your description to check for accuracy.

EXAMINING SIMILARITIES AND DIFFERENCES

Step One: You are going to examine the similarities and differences between two things. What are they called?

Step Two: Can you say some of the ways that they are alike? When you state a way they are alike, give the attribute. For example, if I say that they are both round, the attribute is shape.

Step Three: Can you say some of the ways that they are different? When you state a difference, give the attribute. For example, if I say that this is blue and this is yellow, the attribute is color.

Step Four: Now look at all of the information. Decide what is important and say a few sentences about the two things that you have compared and contrasted.

EXAMINING SIMILARITIES AND DIFFERENCES

Step One: Identify the two things you are examining.

Step Two: Identify similarities between the two things, the attribute of each similarity, and how each similarity is significant. For example, if I say that they are both round, the attribute is shape.

Step Three: Identify the differences between the two things, the attribute of each difference, and explain how each difference is significant. For example, if I say that this is blue and this is yellow, the attribute is color.

Step Four: Use the similarities, differences, and their significance to state an interpretation or summary regarding the two things.

ANALYZING THE PARTS OF A WHOLE

Step One: Name the object.

Step Two: Name the different parts of the object.

Step Three: Choose a part of the object and talk about what the part does and what would happen if that part were not there. Repeat for all the important parts.

Step Four: Say a few sentences about the object and its parts.

ANALYZING THE PARTS OF A WHOLE

Step One: Identify the whole.

Step Two: Identify the parts of the whole.

Step Three: For each part, identify its function and what would happen if that part were not there.

Step Four: Use all the information to state an interpretation or summary to describe how the parts contribute to the whole.

CATEGORIZING

Step One: What are you sorting?

Step Two: What are the categories that you are using to sort the items? What are the characteristics of the category?

Step Three: Place each of the items into the best category and explain why you have chosen that category.

Step Four: In a few sentences, say something about what you did.

CATEGORIZING

Step One: Identify what you are sorting.

Step Two: Identify the categories into which the objects can be placed and the characteristics for each category.

Step Three: Consider each item and describe its characteristics. Place each item and explain why you chose that category.

Step Four: Use all the information to state an interpretation or summary about the items and categories and what you have learned by categorizing in this way.

GROUPING

Step One: Look at each item and describe it.

Step Two: Say some ways you could group them. What would your categories be?

Step Three: In a few sentences, say something about what you did.

Step Four: Now Categorize the items.

GROUPING

Step One: Consider each object and describe its characteristics.

Step Two: Identify possible groupings that you could use and explain the significance of grouping this way.

Step Three: State an interpretation or summary about the grouping you are going to use.

Step Four: Group the items using the Structured Thinking Skill of Categorizing.

ORDERING BY TIME

Step One: Describe what you are ordering.

Step Two: Place the events in order and explain what you are doing.

Step Three: In a few sentences, say something about when the events happened.

ORDERING BY TIME

Step One: Identify what you are ordering and why.

Step Two: Identify the type of ordering that fits this purpose.

Step Three: Place the events or actions in order according to the interval of time in which they happened or you expect them to happen.

Step Four: Use all the information to state an interpretation or summary regarding the significance of the order.

ORDERING BY OCCURRENCE

Step One: Describe what you are ordering.

Step Two: Place the events or actions in order. Talk about the relationship between the steps. What would happen if you skipped a step?

Step Three: In a few sentences, say something about the order of the events.

ORDERING BY OCCURRENCE

Step One: Identify what you are ordering and why.

Step Two: Identify the type of ordering that fits this purpose.

Step Three: Place the events or actions in order and explain the relationship between the steps. Describe what would happen if you omitted a particular step or included one that was incomplete.

Step Four: Use all the information to state an interpretation or summary regarding the significance of the order.

ORDERING BY RANK

Step One: You are going to put these things in order from the_____
to the _____.

Step Two: Place the things in order and give the reasons you ordered
them as you did.

Step Three: In a few sentences, say something about the order and the
ranking.

- OR -

Step One: Describe what you are you placing in order. Say what type
of order you are using.

Step Two: Place the things in order and give the reasons why you
ordered them this way.

Step Three: In a few sentences, say something about the order and the
ranking.

ORDERING BY RANK

Step One: Identify what you are ordering and why.

Step Two: Identify the type of ordering that fits this purpose.

Step Three: Identify the criteria for ranking.

Step Four: Place the items in order according to how they meet the
criteria. State the reasons.

Step Five: Use all the information to state an interpretation or
summary regarding the significance of the order.

SUPPORTING A CONCLUSION:
EXAMINING AN AUTHOR'S CONCLUSION

Step One: What do you think is the author's conclusion?

Step Two: List all the reasons that you can find.

Step Three: What do you think about the author's conclusion?

SUPPORTING A CONCLUSION:
EXAMINING AN AUTHOR'S CONCLUSION

Step One: State the author's conclusion.

Step Two: Find and list the support given in the text for this conclusion.

Step Three: Identify any unstated reasons or assumptions the author may be using to support the conclusion.

Step Four: State an interpretation or summary regarding the author's conclusion and support.

SUPPORTING A CONCLUSION:
EXAMINING MY OWN CONCLUSION

Step One: In a few sentences, say something about what you have seen or read.

Step Two: List your support for saying that.

Step Three: Say something about your conclusion.

SUPPORTING A CONCLUSION:
EXAMINING MY OWN CONCLUSION

Step One: State a conclusion about what you have seen or read.

Step Two: Find and list the support given in the text for this conclusion.

Step Three: Identify any unstated assumptions related to your support.

Step Four: State an interpretation or summary regarding your conclusion and support.

STRUCTURED THINKING SKILL MASTERY

MASTERY OF THE SKILL
WILL RESULT IN STUDENTS BEING ABLE TO:

- Name the skill and state how they are using it. For example, "I am using the skill of Examining Similarities and Differences to develop my understanding of hurricanes and tornadoes."

- Name the mental steps of the skill.

- Explain which step they are using.

- Attempt every step of the skill.

- Explain what their thinking and their summary statement would lack if they skipped any step.

- Listen and respond to other group members.

DEFINING

MASTERY OF THE SKILL WILL RESULT IN STUDENTS BEING ABLE TO:

- Name the skill and state how they are using it. For example, "I am using the Structured Thinking Skill of Defining to develop my understanding of different types of triangles."

- Name the mental steps in the skill:

  Step One: Name the large category to which the item belongs.

  Step Two: State enough defining attributes to set the item apart from every other member of the category.

  Use this question as a check: "Have I identified enough attributes to set it apart from all other members of the group?" If not, state more attributes.

  Step Three: State a definition.

- Explain which step they are using.

- Attempt every step of the skill.

- Explain what their thinking and their summary statement would lack if they skipped any step.

  Listen and respond to other group members.

DESCRIBING

MASTERY OF THE SKILL
WILL RESULT IN STUDENTS BEING ABLE TO:

- Name the skill and state how they are using it. For example, "I am using the Structured Thinking Skill of Describing to develop my understanding of giraffes."

- Name the mental steps in the skill:

  Step One: State the purpose of the description, i.e., humor, explanation, insight, inspiration, or aesthetic.

  Step Two: Create a mental picture of the item.

  Step Three: Verbalize the attributes of each item: size, shape, color, texture, smell, sound, etc.

  Step Four: Verbalize how each attribute is significant, using analogies or making connections with prior knowledge.

  Step Five: Add details by developing words and phrases that accurately communicate your mental picture to others.

  Step Six: Restate or read your description to check for accuracy.

- Explain which step they are using.

- Attempt to do every step of the skill.

- Explain what their thinking and their conclusion would lack if they skipped any step.

- Listen and respond to other group members.

EXAMINING SIMILARITIES AND DIFFERENCES

MASTERY OF THE SKILL
WILL RESULT IN STUDENTS BEING ABLE TO:

- Name the skill and state how it is being used. For example, "I am using the Structured Thinking Skill of Examining Similarities and Differences to develop my understanding of hurricanes and tornadoes."

- Name the mental steps of the skill:

  Step One: Identify the two things you are examining.

  Step Two: Identify similarities between the two things, the attribute of each similarity, and how each similarity is significant. For example, if I say that they are both round, the attribute is shape.

  Step Three: Identify the differences between the two things, the attribute of each difference, and explain how each difference is significant. For example, if I say that this is blue and this is yellow, the attribute is color.

  Step Four: Use the similarities, differences, and their significance to state an interpretation or summary regarding the two objects.

- Explain which step they are using.

- Attempt every step of the skill.

- Explain what their thinking and their summary statement would lack if they skipped any step.

- Listen and respond to other group members.

ANALYZING THE PARTS OF A WHOLE

MASTERY OF THE SKILL
WILL RESULT IN STUDENTS BEING ABLE TO:

- Name the skill and state how they are using it. For example, "I am using the Structured Thinking Skill of Analyzing the Parts of a Whole to develop my understanding of the different sections of a symphony orchestra."

- Name the mental steps in the skill:

  Step One: Identify the whole.

  Step Two: Identify the parts of the whole.

  Step Three: For each part, identify its function and what would happen if that part were not there.

  Step Four: Use all the information to state an interpretation or summary to describe how the parts contribute to the whole.

- Explain which step they are using.

- Attempt every step of the skill.

- Explain what their thinking and their summary statement would lack if they skipped any step.

- Listen and respond to other group members.

CATEGORIZING

MASTERY OF THE SKILL
WILL RESULT IN STUDENTS BEING ABLE TO:

- Name the skill and state how they are using it. For example, "I am using the Structured Thinking Skill of Categorizing to develop my understanding of different types of triangles."

- Name the mental steps in the skill:

  Step One: Identify what you are sorting.

  Step Two: Identify the categories into which the objects can be placed and the characteristics for each category.

  Step Three: Consider each item and describe its characteristics. Place each item and explain why you chose that category.

  Step Four: Use all the information to state an interpretation or summary about the items and categories and what have you learned by categorizing in this way.

- Explain which step they are using.

- Attempt every step of the skill.

- Explain what their thinking and their summary statement would lack if they skipped any step.

- Listen and respond to other group members.

GROUPING

MASTERY OF THE SKILL
WILL RESULT IN STUDENTS BEING ABLE TO:

- Name the skill and state how they are using it. For example, "I am using the Structured Thinking Skill of Grouping to develop my understanding of different types of triangles."

- Name the mental steps in the skill:

  Step One: Consider each object and describe its characteristics.

  Step Two: Identify possible groupings that you could use and explain the significance of grouping this way.

  Step Three: State an interpretation or summary about the grouping you are going to use.

  Step Four: Group the items using the Structured Thinking Skill of Categorizing.

- Explain which step they are using.

- Attempt every step of the skill.

- Explain what their thinking and their summary statement would lack if they skipped any step.

- Listen and respond to other group members.

ORDERING BY TIME

MASTERY OF THE SKILL
WILL RESULT IN STUDENTS BEING ABLE TO:

- Name the skill and state how they are using it. For example, "I am using the Structured Thinking Skill of Ordering by Time to develop my understanding of events that led up to the Cuban Missile Crisis."

- Name the mental steps in the skill:

    Step One: Identify what you are ordering and why.

    Step Two: Identify the type of ordering that fits this purpose.

    Step Three: Place the events or actions in order according to the interval of time in which they happened or you expect them to happen.

    Step Four: Use all the information to state an interpretation or summary regarding the significance of the order.

- Explain which step they are using.

- Attempt every step of the skill.

- Explain what their thinking and their summary statement would lack if they skipped any step.

- Listen and respond to other group members.

ORDERING BY OCCURRENCE

**MASTERY OF THE SKILL
WILL RESULT IN STUDENTS BEING ABLE TO:**

- Name the skill and state how they are using it. For example, "I am using the Structured Thinking Skill of Ordering by Occurrence to develop my understanding of the life cycle of a butterfly."

- Name the mental steps in the skill:

  Step One: Identify what you are ordering and why.

  Step Two: Identify the type of ordering that fits this purpose.

  Step Three: Place the events or actions in order and explain the relationship between the steps. Describe what would happen if you omitted a particular step or included one that was incomplete.

  Step Four: Use all the information to state an interpretation or summary regarding the significance of the order.

- Explain which step they are using.

- Attempt every step of the skill.

- Explain what their thinking and their summary statement would lack if they skipped any step.

- Listen and respond to other group members.

ORDERING BY RANK

MASTERY OF THE SKILL
WILL RESULT IN STUDENTS BEING ABLE TO:

- Name the skill and state how they are using it. For example, "I am using the Structured Thinking Skill of Ordering by Rank to develop my understanding of the relationship of the population size of these cities."

- Name the mental steps in the skill as follows:

  Step One: Identify what you are ordering and why.

  Step Two: Identify the type of ordering that fits this purpose.

  Step Three: Identify the criteria for ranking.

  Step Four: Place the items in order according to how they meet the criteria. State the reasons.

  Step Five: Use all the information to state an interpretation or summary regarding the significance of the order.

- Explain which step they are using.

- Attempt every step of the skill.

- Explain what their thinking and their summary statement would lack if they skipped any step.

- Listen and respond to other group members.

SUPPORTING A CONCLUSION: EXAMINING MY OWN CONCLUSION

MASTERY OF THE SKILL WILL RESULT IN STUDENTS BEING ABLE TO:

- Name the skill and state how they are using it. For example, "I am using the Structured Thinking Skill of Supporting a Conclusion: Examining My Own Conclusion to respond to 'Of Revenge' by Bacon."

- Name the mental steps in the skill:

  Step One: State a conclusion about what you have seen or read.

  Step Two: Find and list the support given in the text for this conclusion.

  Step Three: Identify any unstated assumptions related to your support.

  Step Four: State an interpretation or summary regarding your conclusion and support.

- Explain which step they are using.

- Attempt every step of the skill

- Explain what their thinking and their summary statement would lack if they skipped any step.

- Listen and respond to other group members.

SUPPORTING A CONCLUSION: EXAMINING AN AUTHOR'S CONCLUSION

MASTERY OF THE SKILL WILL RESULT IN STUDENTS BEING ABLE TO:

- Name the skill and state how they are using it. For example, "I am using the Structured Thinking Skill of Supporting a Conclusion: Examining an Author's Conclusion to respond to this editorial promoting the inclusion of fluoride in drinking water."

- Name the mental steps in the skill:

  Step One: State the author's conclusion.

  Step Two: Find and list the support given in the text for this conclusion.

  Step Three: Identify any unstated reasons or assumptions the author may be using to support the conclusion.

  Step Four: State an interpretation or summary regarding the author's conclusion and support

- Explain which step they are using.

- Attempt every step of the skill.

- Explain what their thinking and their summary statement would lack if they skipped any step.

- Listen and respond to other group members.

APPENDIX C

Classroom Integration of VESC™ Strategies

VESC™ LESSON PLAN

SCHOOL:	
NAME:	
SUBJECT:	
CONTENT AREA:	
GRADE LEVEL:	
STANDARDS ADDRESSED:	
ASSESSMENT:	
HOMEWORK:	
LESSON:	

IMPLEMENTATION SCHEDULE

WEEK	NEW VESC™ STRATEGIES PRESENTED IN TEACHER WORKSHOP	CLASSROOM INTRODUCTION OF VESC™ STRATEGIES	CLASSROOM PRACTICE OF VESC™ STRATEGIES

VESC™ UNIT PLAN

SUBJECT AREA:
CONTENT UNIT:
STANDARDS:

CONTENT OBJECTIVES (Students will be able to...)	TYPE OF THINKING NEEDED TO RESPOND	LESSON USING VESC™ STRATEGIES AND CONTENT SPECIFICS	STUDENT PRODUCTS AND ACTIVITIES

UNIT RESOURCES AND TECHNOLOGY INTEGRATION:

STUDENT PRIOR KNOWLEDGE SELF-ASSESSMENT

CONTENT UNIT:

QUESTIONS TO ASK YOURSELF	YES	NO
Can I define and describe the topic?		
Can I group the topic into categories?		
Can I divide the topic into parts and verbalize the function of each part?		
Can I order any processes that relate to the topic?		
Can I examine the similarities and differences of items related to the topic?		
Which Structured Thinking Skills could I use to learn more about this topic?		

STUDENT END-OF-UNIT
SELF-ASSESSMENT ACTIVITIES

CONTENT UNIT:	
Define and describe the topic.	
Group the topic into categories.	
Divide the topic into parts and verbalize the function of each part.	
Order any processes that relate to the topic	
Examine similarities and differences of items related to the topic.	
Which Structured Thinking Skills did I use to understand this topic?	

THE VESC™ CLASSROOM

Teacher's Role	Student's Role
TALKING ALOUD PAIRED PROBLEM SOLVING	
• provide the guidelines for effective verbalization of thinking • provide the guidelines for effective listening • demonstrate how to separate my thinking from the thinking of the Problem Solver • assess each student	• practice speaking coherently whenever I am in the classroom • practice active listening • ask questions when I do not understand the Problem Solver • practice separating my thinking from the thinking of the Problem Solver • assess my ability to verbalize thinking
EFFECTIVE GROUP PROCESS	
• provide the guidelines for Effective Group Process • schedule practice sessions to learn Effective Group Process • expect the rules of Effective Group Process to be practiced by all students in the classroom • expect each student to self-correct behavior	• practice the guidelines of Effective Group Process daily • self-correct my behavior when I forget the guidelines of Effective Group Process • self-correct my behavior without disrupting the learning process • enter into the practice sessions for learning Effective Group Process • assess my ability to engage in Effective Group Process
STRUCTURED THINKING	
• raise my awareness of the type of thinking I am to use in the activity • teach the mental steps to use when using the Structured Thinking Skill • provide reference information to use • facilitate my use of the thinking skill • clarify reference information I do not understand	• become aware of my thinking • learn the mental steps I use to independently organize the information • use reference information to identify facts • organize facts according to the mental steps • assess facts for meaning • communicate the meaning of information • clarify information as I progress through the mental steps • ask questions when I do not understand

Name: _____

DIRECTIONS: Read the following paragraph and answer the questions using complete sentences for your answers.

MOLEK SIOLUS

Because the molek siolus fract controls sactions that involve coctrans, warkes, and oplors, it has been compared to a niosulsus. The circuits of the niosulsus are located throughout the rihfrule. From the moment the niosulsus is manufactured, it is capable of controlling larehs, which are similar to sactions. Since the molek siolus fract controls sactions, which are the major cause of fuhlops, a disruption in the manufacture of the molek siolus fract could be hazardous to puelhs.

1. What does the molek siolus fract control?

2. To what has the molek siolus fract been compared?

3. Where are the circuits of the niosulsus located?

4. The larehs are similar to what other structures?

5. Predict the effect of a disruption in the manufacture of the molek siolus fract.

SUGGESTED READING

Making Connections: Teaching and the Human Brain
Renate and Geoffrey Caine, 1991, Innovative Learning Publications™, USA

Education on the Edge of Possibility
Renate and Geoffrey Caine, 1997, Association for Supervision and Curriculum Development, Alexandria, VA

Control Theory in the Classroom
William Glasser, M.D., 1986 Harper & Row, New York, NY

Emotional Intelligence: Why it can matter more than IQ
Daniel Goleman, 1995, Bantam Books, New York, NY

Working with Emotional Intelligence
Daniel Goleman, 1998, Bantam Books, New York, NY

Discipline and the Disruptive Child
Muriel Schoenbrun Karlin and Regina Berger, 1992, Parker Publishing Company, West Nyack, NY

How To Reach And Teach ADD/ADHD Children
Sandra F. Rief, 1993, The Center for Applied Research in Education, West Nyack, NY

Discipline in the Secondary Classroom: A Problem-by-Problem Survival Guide
Randall S. Sprick, Ph.D., 1995, The Center for Applied Research in Education, West Nyack, NY

Infusing the Teaching of Critical and Creative Thinking Into Content Instruction
Robert Swartz and Sandra Parks, 1994, Critical Thinking Press and Software, Pacific Grove, CA

Infusing the Teaching of Critical and Creative Thinking Into Secondary Science
Robert Swartz, Stephen David Fischer, and Sandra Parks, 1998, Critical Thinking Press and Software, Pacific Grove, CA

Social Skills: Lessons & Activities for Grades 7-12
Ruth Weltman Begun, Editor, 1996, Society for Prevention of Violence, The Center for Applied Research in Education, West Nyack, NY

Notes

Notes

Notes

Notes

Notes

Notes

Notes

Notes